Harnessing Machine Learning for Environmental Restoration and Surveillance

Harnessing Machine Learning for Environmental Restoration and Surveillance is an extensive and comprehensive book, showcasing the applications of machine learning and artificial intelligence in environmental monitoring of the quality of air, soil, and water; prediction of environmental risks; optimization and prediction of remediation processes; and enhancement of resource management.

The book offers readers an opportunity to understand how contemporary smart technology (machine learning and artificial intelligence) can be used to safeguard and improve our environment as well as to solve environmental problems and provide sustainable solutions. It offers insights and an opportunity to evaluate theoretical concepts and real-world case studies, thereby boosting innovation and collaboration. The authors give modest explanations of how artificial intelligence and machine learning can monitor pollution, forecast environmental hazards, and support the optimization process for the effective removal of environmental contaminants. Real-world examples where these advanced smart technology tools have been successfully utilized are also presented in this book.

The content and coverage of this academic text are ideal for undergraduate and postgraduate students, researchers, professionals in environmental science, data science, and engineering, as well as individuals interested in the environment and technology.

Robert Birundu Onyancha is a Senior Lecturer of Physics at the Technical University of Kenya; a Research Fellow at the College of Graduate Studies, School of Interdisciplinary Research and Graduate Studies, University of South Africa; and a Senior Lecturer of Physics on sabbatical at the Department of Physics, School of Pure and Applied Science, Kisii University, Kenya.

Kingsley Eghonghon Ukhurebor is a Senior Lecturer/Researcher (due for an Associate Professor) and acting Director, Centre for Open and Distance Learning and former acting Head of the Department of Physics at Edo State University Iyamho, Nigeria. He is also a Research Fellow at WASCAL, Competence Centre, Ouagadougou, Burkina Faso. His research interests include applied physics, climate physics, environmental physics, telecommunications physics, and materials science (nanotechnology). He is currently ranked among the top 50 authors in Nigeria by Scopus scholarly output and is listed among the top 2% of scientists in the world by Stanford University, USA, and Elsevier.

Uyiosa Osagie Aigbe is a former Research Fellow with the Department of Mathematics and Physics, Faculty of Applied Science, Cape Peninsula University of Technology, Cape Town, South Africa. He was also an Ad-Hoc Research Fellow with the Centre for Space Research and the National Institute of Theoretical and Computational Science, North West University, Potchefstroom, South Africa. He is currently a teaching assistant with the Discipline of Physics, School of Agriculture & Science, College of Agriculture, Engineering & Science, University of KwaZulu-Natal, Pietermaritzburg, South Africa. His research interests are in applied physics, nanotechnology, fluid dynamics, water purification processes, image processing, environmental physics, machine learning, statistical analysis, and materials science.

Harnessing Machine Learning for Environmental Restoration and Surveillance

Robert Birundu Onyancha,
Kingsley Eghonghon Ukhurebor,
and Uyiosa Osagie Aigbe

CRC Press
Taylor & Francis Group
Boca Raton London New York

CRC Press is an imprint of the
Taylor & Francis Group, an **informa** business

Designed cover image: Shutterstock

First edition published 2026
by CRC Press
2385 NW Executive Center Drive, Suite 320, Boca Raton FL 33431

and by CRC Press
4 Park Square, Milton Park, Abingdon, Oxon, OX14 4RN

CRC Press is an imprint of Taylor & Francis Group, LLC

ISBN: 978-1-041-02197-1 (hbk)
ISBN: 978-1-041-02296-1 (pbk)
ISBN: 978-1-003-61858-4 (ebk)

DOI: 10.1201/9781003618584

Typeset in Palatino
by KnowledgeWorks Global Ltd.

Contents

1

Introduction to Environmental Challenges and Technological Solutions

Abstract

Over time, there has been growing concern about the rate at which the environment has continuously degraded. This challenge keeps worsening due to rapid climate change, unchecked pollution, resource depletion, and ecosystem collapse, which now threaten both human life and other life supported by natural systems. It is well known that technological progress has been one of the contributors to these problems through various pathways, such as the burning of fossil fuels, industrialization, rapid urbanization, increased development of infrastructure, increased agricultural activities, and widespread information and communication technology. On the other hand, through existing technology combined with novel and advanced technology that have emerged in the recent past, new systems have been developed and engineered to help address the environmental challenges. This chapter covers major environmental challenges and the role of technology in addressing them. Furthermore, barriers that have hindered the adoption and implementation of various environmental technologies are also discussed. The chapter further offers future directions in environmental impact mitigation.

1.1 Introduction

The use of technology has many advantages in every sector, which has brought a lot of achievements. However, it has an equally negative contribution to environmental degradation, which has threatened human and ecological life (Mancuso, Petruzzelli, Panniello, & Vaia, 2025). It has contributed to climate change, pollution (air, water, and soil), the collapse of biodiversity, the depletion of natural resources, and social inequalities (Figure 1.1). These challenges have been heavily increased by rapid population growth, the development of urban areas, and industrialization, which have led to the untenable usage and consumption of environmental resources (Fletcher et al., 2024; Talaie, Kamyab, & Razmfarsa, 2024). They have threatened human and ecological life and require urgent intervention.

DOI: 10.1201/9781003618584-1

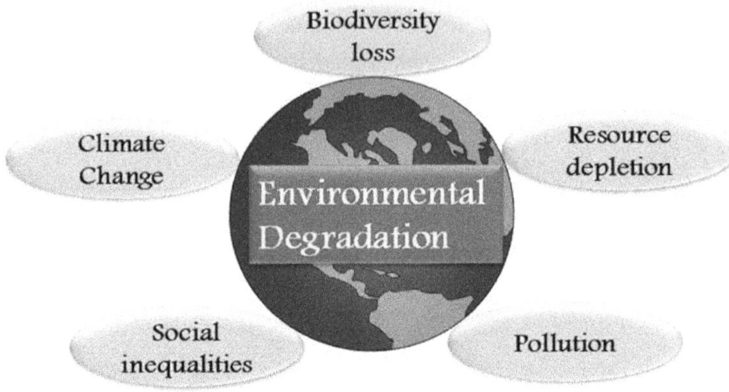

FIGURE 1.1
Representation of contributors to environmental degradation.

It is important to note that the current state of extraction of resources heavily relies on the linear model, where finite resources are extracted and used for production and discarded without optimal usage. Consequently, they produce a huge amount of waste and emission of greenhouse gases (GHGs), which have deepened the degradation of the environment and disrupted the climate patterns. For example, in 2023, the emission of GHG climbed by approximately 1.1% and continued with an upward trend following the COVID-19 recession, with scientists reporting that recent years have been warmer when compared to any other point in the last 125,000 years (Fletcher et al., 2024). These uncertain changes are a risk to agriculture, infrastructure, human life, and ecological systems, while the linear economy of extracting resources leads to depletion of resources, a decline in the supply of essential materials for future generations (Eelager et al., 2023).

Similarly, the continued destruction of natural habitat, combined with the growing pollution and untamed non-ecofriendly practices, has led to the loss of biodiversity. This has weakened the ecosystem, which offers bio-services like the decontamination of water, carbon sequestration, and pollination (Dalbanjan, Kadapure, & Praveen Kumar, 2025; Eelager et al., 2025). Modern imperialism, which is characterized by the extraction of resources and gaining high profits and is protected by a capitalist economy, has been one of the contributing factors. This model has intertwined in the very structure of global relations, thereby influencing how trade is done, dictating and shaping political agendas, and defining the economic strategies of nations worldwide (Fletcher et al., 2024).

The overreliance and continuous extraction of resources to support economies have impeded fundamental progress in nature conservation, decarbonization, and attempts to achieve social equity. For example, in 2022, nearly 4.1 million hectares of primary tropical rainforest were destroyed worldwide, which is 10% more than in 2021. The deforestation released approximately 2.7 Gt of CO_2, which is similar to India's annual emissions from fossil fuel consumption (Fletcher et al., 2024). Similarly, it has been argued that the optimal global population commensurate with the available natural resources should be between 0.5 and 5 billion people (Dasgupta, 2019). Imperatively, the world's population was 8 billion in 2022, and in the next 30 years, it is expected to increase by around 2 billion, reaching about 10.4 billion by 2080 (United Nations, 2024). With the optimal levels known, it therefore implies that any additional person on the planet will disturb agricultural activities and the available resources, leading to the destruction of habitat, rampant pollution, and unmanageable practices, resulting in biodiversity loss due to over-demand of what the biosphere can offer.

Social disparities worsen the situation, with vulnerable communities experiencing the greatest impacts of environmental damage while being denied adequate means to adapt (Ngcamu, 2023). For example, the World Bank Group has indicated that without climate-informed development, tens of millions in the East Asia and Pacific region may fall into extreme poverty by 2030, with the poorest expected to be more exposed to environmental shocks despite the fewer resources to adapt. This solidifies the aspect of economic inequality that perpetuates the climate exposure (World Bank Group, n.d.). Similarly, least developed countries like Burundi, Somalia, and Mozambique, among others, are prone to risks of loss or damage due to climate change, thus reflecting global inequality where those who suffer most are more often than not the least contributors to environmental stressors (International Institute for Environment and Development, 2022). Moreover, studies have shown that the low-income and less educated communities live closer to areas that are exposed to pollution (air, soil, and water), which clearly indicates how the social vulnerability of low income and low education is related to environmental burden (Shen, Wang, & Wang, 2024). Similarly, studies in Los Angeles, California, have shown that areas with less White communities and experiencing lower incomes are exposed to pollution from vehicles even though they often drive less. The study illustrates a systemic inequality in decision-making on roads, freeways, and heavy traffic zones, which tends to disadvantage and burden a set of groups (Boeing, Lu, & Pilgram, 2023).

To address these challenges, an approach is required that can, on the one hand, be involved in reducing, mitigating, and preventing the contributors of environmental degradation, but also, capable of offering engineered innovations and sustainable solutions aimed at restoring the ecosystems (Mancuso et al., 2025). Specifically, striking a balance among three core pillars of the economic advancement, environmental protection, and social well-being is what is well known as sustainability. In reality, it is very challenging to achieve this balance because sustainability issues have always involved multiple stakeholders, with conflicting goals, and difficult trade-offs between economic development and environmental conservation (Acquaye, 2025).

In that regard, quite a number of technologies have been developed and used to manage and improve the environment in order to promote sustainability. For example, low-carbon techniques such as solar photovoltaics, wind, hydropower, geothermal, bioenergy, energy storage (batteries, supercapacitors, fuel cells), and smart grids are increasingly being deployed and have been used in an effort to control and mitigate climate change (Anvari, Medina, Merchán, & Hernández, 2025). In pollution and waste management, different emerging innovations like the use of catalytic converters, membrane filtration, adsorbents, biodegradable materials, smart waste systems, the circular economy, and AI-robotics (where AI is artificial intelligence) sorting have been employed with promising results reported (Fang et al., 2023). Furthermore, the problem of water scarcity has been strengthened through strategies such as desalination, smart irrigation, and water conservation Internet of Things (IoT) systems, while precision farming, vertical farming, and the use of genetically modified crops are now being employed to advance agricultural sustainability (Papadopoulos et al., 2024). To help in limiting urban emissions, smart city models have been adopted, which involve the use of electric vehicles, green buildings, and smart transport systems in various cities (Elassy, Al-Hattab, Takruri, & Badawi, 2024). Finally, the growing availability of environmental data and AI tools has helped in improving decision-making, that is, data-driven decision-making through various applications such as the IoT, geographic information systems (GIS), remote sensing, operations research (OR) modelling, and AI models (Olawade et al., 2024).

Importantly, this aligns well with the global pursuit of an inclusive and sustainable future, which aligns well with the United Nations 2030 Agenda for Sustainable Development. This study is equally related to several Sustainable Development Goals (SDGs), which include the Affordable and Clean Energy (SDG 7); Industry, Innovation, and Infrastructure (SDG 9); Sustainable Cities and Communities (SDG 11); Responsible Consumption and Production (SDG 12); Climate Action (SDG 13); and Life on Land (SDG 15) (Eelager et al., 2025). A critical look at these SDGs only emphasizes the need for a transition from the normal linear economy to a circular-based economic model that encourages and promotes innovation, promotes resource efficiency, and is environmentally friendly (Eelager et al., 2025).

Overall, these technological interventions and advancements demonstrate the progress in using innovations for environmental management and conservation. However, there are still questions regarding their overall effectiveness, integration, and long-term ecological implications. Therefore, this chapter covers major environmental challenges and the role of technology in addressing them. Furthermore, barriers that have hindered the adoption and implementation of various environmental technologies are also discussed. The chapter further offers future directions in environmental impact mitigation. This is achieved through a synthesis of existing published research work that covers the current state of technological innovations that are designed to mitigate environmental challenges and discuss their achievements, critical gaps, barriers, and future research directions.

1.2 Major Environmental Challenges

1.2.1 Climate Change

Climate change is one of the most pressing global problems of the 21st century. The emissions from anthropogenic GHG coming from the burning of fossil fuels, agricultural activities, and deforestation have all increased the concentration of CO_2 to unprecedented levels (Nunes, 2023). This has seen the global mean surface temperature rise by 1.45 ± 0.12°C, which led to a high record of global warming reached in 2023, with an estimate of nearly a third of the global population subjected to fatal heatwaves and wildfires (Fletcher et al., 2024). Notably, studies have projected that the extinction of animals and plants in the next decades will increase by a magnitude of two- to five-fold (Wiens, 2016), with loss of diversity compounded by fragile and unprotected ecosystems [(Díaz et al., 2019; Exposito-Alonso et al., 2022). The consequences of climate change include extreme weather occurrences such as hurricanes, floods, and heatwaves (Ebi et al., 2021), the agricultural sector is facing a shift in rainfall patterns and a reduction in crop yields (Waqas et al., 2025), the warming and acidification of oceans, which threaten the marine biodiversity and fisheries (Venegas, Acevedo, & Treml, 2023), and the rise of sea levels, which has continued to displace people and affect infrastructure (Roy et al., 2023).

1.2.2 Pollution

Pollution in every environmental medium (air, water, and soil) is a universal challenge that needs continuous monitoring, controlling, and mitigating for a safer environment. Air pollution stems from anthropogenic activities such as industrial emissions, burning of fossil fuels, transportation, factory and refinery activities, and power plants, among many more, leading to the production of fine particle matter, nitrogen oxides, sulfur oxides, and ground-level ozone (Manisalidis, Stavropoulou, Stavropoulos, & Bezirtzoglou, 2020). The toxic gases produced and other particles have been associated with cardiovascular conditions, respiratory complications, diseases such as cancer and asthma, and irregularities in the nervous system (Onyancha et al., 2021). Similarly, they have been linked to elevated temperature, which alters the ambient temperature, thus affecting plants, animals, and humans (Onyancha et al., 2021).

Water pollution results from industrial effluents, domestic disposals, microplastics, pharmaceuticals, and agricultural runoffs, which culminate in contamination of rivers, lakes, and oceans. The heavy metals (such as lead, chromium, copper, nickel, etc.), microplastics, dyes, and polyfluoroalkyl substances are especially hazardous due to bioaccumulation (Aigbe et al., 2021; Panieri, Baralic, Djukic-Cosic, Buha Djordjevic, & Saso, 2022; Ukhurebor et al., 2021; Wang et al., 2025). These substances have been found to harm various human organs like the heart, kidneys, liver, throat, and respiratory tract systems, urinary and digestive systems (Onyancha et al., 2022).

Soil pollution is contributed to by unsafe agricultural practices, such as intensive pesticide and fertilizer usage, compounded by mining activities and electronic waste, which contribute heavily to the accumulation of toxic substances in the soils, undermining food safety, affecting agricultural productivity, and endangering living organisms and human beings (Ghazaryan et al., 2024).

1.2.3 Biodiversity Loss and Habitat Degradation

The rapid human impact through deforestation, urbanization, invasive species, pollution, climate change, soil degradation, and overfishing is causing a sixth mass extinction by quickly wiping out biodiversity. This hinders essential ecosystem services, such as pollination, water regulation and treatment, carbon sequestration, and disease control. According to the United Nation's Intergovernmental Science-Policy on Biodiversity and Ecosystem Services (IPBES) report of 2019, around 1 million species (animals and plants) are currently under extinction threat within decades unless urgent and measured action is taken (Watson et al., 2019).

The loss of biodiversity also compromises the resilience of the ecological systems and other systems that support human life. This makes the affected societies to become vulnerable to extreme and hostile conditions or events and also causes the collapse of the ecosystem. Studies have shown that degraded ecosystems resulting from calamities such as wildfires, droughts, and outbreaks of disease have a reduced potential for a full recovery, thus amplifying the effect of climate change on human and natural systems (Abbass et al., 2022).

1.2.4 Resource Depletion

The ever-growing human population, coupled with the expansion of industries, has intensified the harvesting of minerals, fossil fuels, timber, wood, charcoal, and freshwater. Consequently, this has resulted in the diminishing of fish stocks, depletion of the aquifer, soil erosion, pollution, and climate change, among many other issues (Tal, 2025). Furthermore, there is a growing demand for essential resources such as lithium, rare earth elements, and phosphorus, which are continuously being depleted (Kamran, Raugei, & Hutchinson, 2023). It is important to note that these materials are critical in many important fields, like renewable energy technologies, global food production, and electronics. Despite their importance, the extraction has caused serious environmental degradation, loss of biodiversity, and social conflict, particularly in those regions where there are weak regulatory measures (Mangani, Khan, & Ahmad, 2025).

1.2.5 Social Inequality

Social inequality has been one of the challenges that needs to be addressed to ensure fair distribution of environmental benefits and burdens. For example, the construction and implementation of waste management facilities or the siting of industrial projects may have been found to impact low-income neighbourhoods, which reaffirms the notion that certain environmental policies excessively affect marginalized communities, leading to environmental injustices (Islam, 2024). Furthermore, a shift in mindset is needed to fight resistance to change at individual and institutional levels in the adoption of technology. To overcome this, technological innovation and effective communication, education, and policy incentives to shift attitudes and behaviours towards a more sustainable mindset must be encouraged (Ezeigweneme, Daraojimba, Tula, Adegbite, & Gidiagba, 2024).

Also, promoting social equity through providing equal access to education and healthcare will not only empower individuals but also reduce inequalities and drive innovations (Mamun & Alam, 2025). Also, fair and equitable allocation and distribution of essential utilities such as clean water, access to food, and energy can help reduce the structural vulnerabilities that have always made disadvantaged groups more vulnerable to environmental problems. Furthermore, when marginalized groups are included in decision-making, they feel a sense of involvement, which can be one of the ways of addressing systemic barriers (Summers et al., 2024). This can be done together with the involvement of those communities that are underrepresented to ensure that the use of technology and solving environmental problems reflect the diverse needs and local realities. Another very important aspect that can be advocated to reduce inequality is economic inclusion, which can be championed through microfinance, vocational training, and social entrepreneurship, which will help bridge the perennial gaps that have been existing and foster shared prosperity.

1.3 Traditional and Emerging Technological Solutions

1.3.1 Renewable Energy and Decarbonization Technologies

One of the ways of addressing climate change is through the use of renewable energy. This can be achieved through various energy technologies like solar photovoltaics (Sampaio & González, 2017), wind turbines (Shoaib, Siddiqui, Rehman, Khan, & Alhems, 2019), hydropower (Kaygusuz, 2016), geothermal energy (Moya, Aldás, & Kaparaju, 2018), and bioenergy (Singh, Sarkar, & Dutta, 2022). The adoption of these technologies has seen a reduction in the over-reliance on fossil fuels, which has resulted in reduced GHG emissions, thus leading to energy independence. Apart from the generation of energy, it's important to embrace complementary technologies like energy storage systems, smart grids, and carbon capture. The essence of energy storage systems is to store energy and ensure a continuous supply, which addresses the intermittent energy issues from renewable sources (Amir et al., 2023). This has resulted in the development of batteries such as lithium batteries and sodium, supercapacitors, and fuel cell technologies, which have transformed various industries and, more importantly, reduced over-reliance on finite natural resources from the environment (Lobato-Peralta, Okoye, & Alegre, 2024). Likewise, with the advent of new and advanced materials such as perovskite for solar cells and hybrid composites for next-generation batteries, renewable energy is projected to be more accessible and affordable (Afroz, Ratnesh, Srivastava, & Singh, 2025).

Similarly, green building and sustainable transport technologies in the construction and transport industries, respectively, are massively contributing to environmental management and sustainability. It is imperative to note that the construction industry is one of the drivers that has contributed heavily to resource extraction from the environment and global emissions. The adoption of green building technologies in developing constructions offers an efficient energy strategy that is environmentally friendly and sustainable (Jaradat, Alshboul, Obeidat, & Zoubi, 2024). On the other hand, it is evident that quite a significant amount of global emissions emanates from the transport sector. Therefore, with the introduction of electric vehicles and the expansion of electric charging infrastructures, the population will be encouraged to use public transport and appreciate the use of intelligent transport systems, which will significantly reduce the over-dependence of internal combustion engines (Sarda et al., 2024).

1.3.2 Pollution Control and Waste Management

The effects of air, soil, and water pollution, combined with poor waste management, have also been another threat to the environment and human welfare. For instance, a high percentage of water contamination comes from anthropogenic activities, where discharges from households, industries, and factories are allowed to flow into water systems (Onyancha et al., 2022). As a result, various water treatment and remediation strategies such as adsorption, desalination, catalytic converters, emission control systems, and membrane filtration have been employed to remove or reduce pollutants and enhance water quality (Balaram, Copia, Kumar, Miller, & Chidambaram, 2023). Also, through material science, engineering, and green chemistry, new and environmentally friendly solvents, adsorbents, and biodegradable materials have been produced and used in water treatment technologies (Aigbe et al., 2021; Neolaka et al., 2022). On the other hand, to reduce wastage of water as a scarce resource, the population has been encouraged to embrace smart irrigation, enhance monitoring, and water conservation methodologies in agricultural and urban settings to ensure proper water management (Kumar et al., 2024). Another important strategy to address waste management is through the circular economy, which emphasizes waste minimization by encouraging sorting, recycling, upcycling, and eco-industrial collaboration (Eelager et al., 2023). Furthermore, with the emergence of AI and robotics in the production chain, there has been an introduction to automation in sorting and optimization, which has offered a good platform to improve recycling efficiency and maximize waste-to-energy conversion (Olawade et al., 2024).

1.3.3 Precision Agriculture and Biotechnology

To improve production in the agricultural sector while minimizing environmental degradation, precision agriculture, which employs systems like drones, satellite imaging, and IoT sensors, has been used with a clear aim of optimizing the irrigation systems, helping in the application of fertilizer, and controlling pests (Mamabolo et al., 2025). Equally, there has been an encouragement to embrace vertical farming as opposed to the traditional agricultural methods, which have been accelerating environmental degradation through deforestation. Also, to address issues affecting crops such as drought and pests, genetically modified crops with enhanced drought and pest resistance have been developed, which have the potential to reduce the application of chemicals and pesticide usage and water consumption (Raman, 2017).

1.3.4 Data and Data-Driven Tools

Different technological innovations that are data-driven, such as IoT, GIS, and remote sensing, have been used to monitor and record real-time ecological variables (Narayana et al., 2024). This is similar to the smart city programs that employ the same tools in water and waste systems, transport, and energy sectors, with a clear focus on enhancing efficiency and minimizing emissions (Russo, 2025). Similarly, the use of operations research (OR) to offer data-driven insights has been on the rise. The technique integrates the data obtained from systems like IoT, GIS, and remote sensing and applies mathematical models. It has been used to optimize, analyze, and offer predictions on how resources are used and to determine ecological impacts (Acquaye, 2025).

Likewise, AI has been employed in environmental science to good effect through the offering of data-driven insights that have helped stakeholders in decision-making (Bolón-Canedo, Morán-Fernández, Cancela, &

Alonso-Betanzos, 2024). For instance, AI has shaped how environmental issues are investigated, monitored, and addressed by using its ability to process and analyse huge datasets. It is good to note that conventional strategies such as statistical analysis, regression models, empirical correlations, and manual monitoring methods have been found to suffer from drawing accurate insights from environmental data due to the scale of the datasets, heterogeneity, and complexity. However, AI technologies, specifically machine learning (ML), natural language processing (NLP), and neural networks (NN), are capable of identifying patterns in data, performing accurate predictions, and offering optimization (Olawade et al., 2024). For example, ML has been employed to predict air pollution, evaluate water quality, and optimize waste management systems (Alsabt, Alkhaldi, Adenle, & Alshuwaikhat, 2024; Zhu et al., 2022), with NN models being reliably used to enhance the precision of weather forecasts and GHG emission predictions (Antanasijević, Ristić, Perić-Grujić, & Pocajt, 2014). Similarly, NLP techniques have been utilized to analyse environmental documentation, extract critical insights, and offer evidence-based decision-making that can guide in crafting good policy and resource management (Talaie et al., 2024).

1.4 Challenges in Technology Implementation

1.4.1 Economic Barriers

Most of the technologies, such as renewable energy, advanced wastewater treatment systems, waste management smart grid technologies, and AI-driven, are capital-intensive. This limits and disadvantages developing countries and regions due to limited access to financial aid, subsidies, and incentives, hence challenging their adoption (Panja, Paul, & Jha, 2025). For example, in renewable energy, the cost of solar photovoltaics and wind power has remained relatively cheap, but the prices of the storage technologies remain expensive (Osman et al., 2023). Also, there has always been uncertainty and unpredictability of the market, which, when compounded by short-term horizons, tends to discourage private investors from engaging and financing projects that have a long period of tenure (Demirel, Leendertse, & Volker, 2022). Apart from the initial capital, low-income countries face challenges such as limited credit facilities, high interest rates, and weak institutional frameworks, which have contributed to the slow uptake of modern environmental technologies (Nasim, Chen, al Najjar, & Hoang, 2025). Another barrier is the high overhead maintenance and operational costs resulting from the need to have specialized and trained personnel and stable energy (Sorrell, Mallett, & Nye, 2011). Furthermore, the other challenges are centered around intellectual property, over-reliance on the skills, and experience from foreign engineering firms, instead of offering training to the local population (Tsani, Chitou, & Overland, 2024).

1.4.2 Social Inequality

Social inequalities are another big contributor to the slow adoption of technology, more specifically in marginalized communities. For instance, there has always been unequal access to clean technologies like water purification, renewable energy, precision and smart agriculture, which draws a big contrast between the wealthy and the marginalized societies. Lack of information, education, and technical capacity in rural areas has equally delayed the acceptance of new technologies (Kapucu, Ge, Rott, & Isgandar, 2024).

Furthermore, social inequalities have also been found to influence the adoption of a technology governance structure (Ho & Ho, 2025). For instance, it has been reported that marginalized communities often experience a lack of participation in making decisions that are related to technology. This leads to the loss of a sense of ownership, reduced confidence in the new technology systems, and hence slow uptake. Studies have revealed that if communities have been excluded from planning and developing policies on a particular system, they have been found to be less likely to adopt and implement it, even when the system is meant to benefit them (Nirmani, 2025). Also, participation in technological innovation has always been discouraged by a huge difference in digital connectivity, such as poor internet connections, expensive data costs, and intermittent power supply (Nirmani, 2025).

1.4.3 Technical Limitations

One of the biggest limitations to AI is the availability of large-scale datasets that are of high quality for training, testing, and validating ML and deep learning. The reality shows that the environmental data that is available is sparse, inconsistent, and highly fragmented. Similarly, the technologies employed in environmental systems, such as IoT, GIS, and other sensors, lack standardized and interoperability mechanisms, which makes the integration and comparison across different platforms and regions very difficult (Rolnick et al., 2022).

Furthermore, ML models require high-computing infrastructure, which is a big challenge in many regions that have strained resources. Also, ML models often suffer from generalization when developed on specific geographical or ecological datasets and are used on other systems whose variables continuously vary. In addition, ML models operate as "black boxes" while the environmental processes are always complex and nonlinear. These make interpretability difficult and hence restrict the adoption by policymakers who always require straightforward, transparent, and easily explainable insights that can help in decision-making (Yazici, Shayea, & Din, 2023).

1.4.4 Ethical and Governance Barriers

The introduction of new technologies like AI presents ethical dilemmas and governance gaps. For example, the use of satellite or drone monitoring in areas that overlap human settlements raises privacy concerns (Resnik & Elliott, 2019). Similarly, it has been established that ML suffers from algorithmic bias, which can lead to misinformation and misrepresentation of environmental risks, thereby resulting in under-allocation and misallocation of resources (Nazer et al., 2023). Also, the use of genetically modified crops and bioenergy crops can lead to conflict in land use and loss of biodiversity by displacing natural ecosystems, reducing crop rotation, and increasing the demand for land, which will possibly alter local ecosystems (Chowdhury, Mahi, Yeassin, Chowdhury, & Farrok, 2025).

1.4.5 Policy Constraints

The implementation and usage of technology often face inconsistent regulations, coupled with weak enforcement and a lack of local and international coordination and support (Pittri, Godawatte, Esangbedo, Antwi-Afari, & Bao, 2025). Also, the rate of technological evolution has always outpaced regulatory formulations and adaptation, which creates uncertainty when it comes to usage in industries and communities (Pittri, Godawatte, Esangbedo, Antwi-Afari, & Bao, 2025). Furthermore, insufficient funding for programs and the unavailability of a clear policy on how to provide incentives to encourage the uptake and adoption of technology are big challenges. Similarly, many low-income and developing countries don't have robust and well-structured governance systems, which then translates into having inadequate personnel, poor oversight, and insignificant engagement of stakeholders when making decisions. Additionally, failure to have policies that address data governance issues that include ownership of the data, privacy, and security is of major concern since these issues are critical in IoT and IA applications (Smidt & Jokonya, 2022).

1.5 Conclusion and Future Prospects

There has been an urgent call to address contemporary environmental challenges amid the rising population, industrialization, and urbanization in order to safeguard the environment and ensure a continued support for ecological lives. These can be achieved through innovation, collaboration, and ensuring that there is shared global responsibility. Importantly, the use of old and emerging technologies as a tool to solve the growing threat of pollution, depletion of resources, loss of biodiversity, climate change, and social inequalities has made a tremendous contribution. Although there are limitations attached to the available technologies, this opens new platforms for continued improvement and transformation aimed at achieving a sustainable environment for all.

For example, technological advancement in areas such as renewable energy, energy storage, and smart agriculture has the potential to enhance the quality and quantity of production while conserving the environment. Similarly, the implementation of the circular economy should be encouraged to ensure reduced wastage, conservation of resources, and minimization of environmental degradation. Furthermore, there is a serious need to establish policy innovation and advocate for international collaboration to address issues around sustainable practices, green economy, and the prioritization of long-term environmental health that is long-term. Another important aspect is ensuring sustainable financing and investment models are created to encourage businesses to align their daily operations and long-term operations with environmentally set goals. In addition, the public must be empowered through awareness, education, and training on issues of environmental mitigation to ensure.

References

Abbass, K., Qasim, M., Song, H., Murshed, M., Mahmood, H., & Younis, I. (2022). A review of the global climate change impacts, adaptation, and sustainable mitigation measures. *Environmental Science and Pollution Research, 29*(28), 42539–42559.

Acquaye, A. (2025). Operational research for sustainability: A synthesis of methods, applications and challenges. *Journal of the Operational Research Society, 77*(1) 8–42. https://doi.org/10.1080/01605682.2025.2523362

Afroz, M., Ratnesh, R., Srivastava, S., & Singh, J. (2025). Perovskite solar cells: Progress, challenges, and future avenues to clean energy. *Solar Energy, 287,* 113205.

Aigbe, U., Ukhurebor, K., Onyancha, R., Osibote, O., Darmokoesoemo, H., & Kusuma, H. (2021). Fly ash-based adsorbent for adsorption of heavy metals and dyes from aqueous solution: A review. *Journal of Materials Research and Technology, 14,* 2751–2774.

Alsabt, R., Alkhaldi, W., Adenle, Y., & Alshuwaikhat, H. (2024). Optimizing waste management strategies through artificial intelligence and machine learning – An economic and environmental impact study. *Cleaner Waste Systems, 8,* 100158.

Amir, M., Deshmukh, R., Khalid, H., Said, Z., Raza, A., Muyeen, S., ... Sopian, K. (2023). Energy storage technologies: An integrated survey of developments, global economical/environmental effects, optimal scheduling model, and sustainable adaption policies. *Journal of Energy Storage, 72,* 108694.

Antanasijević, D., Ristić, M., Perić-Grujić, A., & Pocajt, V. (2014). Forecasting GHG emissions using an optimized artificial neural network model based on correlation and principal component analysis. *International Journal of Greenhouse Gas Control, 20,* 244–253.

Anvari, S., Medina, A., Merchán, R., & Hernández, A. (2025). Sustainable solar/biomass/energy storage hybridization for enhanced renewable energy integration in multi-generation systems: A comprehensive review. *Renewable and Sustainable Energy Reviews. 223*. 115997. https://doi.org/10.1016/j.rser.2025.115997

Balaram, V., Copia, L., Kumar, U., Miller, J., & Chidambaram, S. (2023). Pollution of water resources and application of ICP-MS techniques for monitoring and management – A comprehensive review. *Geosystems and Geoenvironment, 2*(4), 100210.

Boeing, G., Lu, Y., & Pilgram, C. (2023). Local inequities in the relative production of and exposure to vehicular air pollution in Los Angeles. *Urban Studies, 60*(12), 2351–2368.

Bolón-Canedo, V., Morán-Fernández, L., Cancela, B., & Alonso-Betanzos, A. (2024). A review of green artificial intelligence: Towards a more sustainable future. *Neurocomputing, 599*, 128096.

Chowdhury, P., Mahi, N., Yeassin, R., Chowdhury, N., & Farrok, O. (2025). Biomass to biofuel: Impacts and mitigation of environmental, health, and socioeconomic challenges. *Energy Conversion and Management, 25*, 100889.

Dalbanjan, N., Kadapure, A., & Praveen Kumar, S. (2025). Stress-induced proteins enhance thermal endurance in soil bacterium Priestia aryabhattai strain PSK. N2. *Antonie Van Leeuwenhoek, 118*(8), 102.

Dasgupta, P. (2019). *Time and the generations: Population ethics for a diminishing planet.* New York, NY: Columbia University Press.

Demirel, H., Leendertse, W., & Volker, L. (2022). Mechanisms for protecting returns on private investments in public infrastructure projects. *International Journal of Project Management, 40*(3), 155–166.

Díaz, S., Settele, J., Brondízio, E., Ngo, H., Agard, J., Arneth, A., … Garibaldi, L. (2019). Pervasive human-driven decline of life on Earth points to the need for transformative change. *Science, 366*(6471), eaax3100.

Ebi, K., Vanos, J., Baldwin, J., Bell, J., Hondula, D., Errett, N., … Berry, P. (2021). Extreme weather and climate change: Population health and health system implications. *Annual Review of Public Health, 42*(1), 293–315.

Eelager, M., Dalbanjan, N., Madihalli, S., Madar, M., Agadi, N., Korganokar, K., & Kiran, B. (2025). Pathways to a sustainable future: Exploring the synergy between sustainability and circular economy. *Sustainable Futures, 10*, 101208.

Eelager, M., Masti, S., Chougale, R., Hiremani, V., Narasgoudar, S., Dalbanjan, N., & SK, P. (2023). Evaluation of mechanical, antimicrobial, and antioxidant properties of vanillic acid induced chitosan/poly (vinyl alcohol) active films to prolong the shelf life of green chilli. *International Journal of Biological Macromolecules, 232*, 123499.

Elassy, M., Al-Hattab, M., Takruri, M., & Badawi, S. (2024). Intelligent transportation systems for sustainable smart cities. *Transportation Engineering, 16*, 100252.

Exposito-Alonso, M., Booker, T., Czech, L., Gillespie, L., Hateley, S., Kyriazis, C., … Ruffley, M. (2022). Genetic diversity loss in the Anthropocene. *Science, 377*(6613), 1431–1435.

Ezeigweneme, C., Daraojimba, C., Tula, O., Adegbite, A., & Gidiagba, J. (2024). A review of technological innovations and environmental impact mitigation. *World Journal of Advanced Research and Reviews, 21*(1), 075–082.

Fang, B., Yu, J., Chen, Z., Osman, A., Farghali, M., Ihara, I., … Yap, P. (2023). Artificial intelligence for waste management in smart cities: A review. *Environmental Chemistry Letters, 21*(4), 1959–1989.

Fletcher, C., Ripple, W., Newsome, T., Barnard, P., Beamer, K., Behl, A., … Hiser, K. (2024). Earth at risk: An urgent call to end the age of destruction and forge a just and sustainable future. *PNAS Nexus, 3*(4), 106.

Ghazaryan, K., Agrawal, S., Margaryan, G., Harutyunyan, A., Rajput, P., Movsesyan, H., … Alwahibi, M. (2024). Soil pollution: An agricultural and environmental problem with nanotechnological remediation opportunities and challenges. *Discover Sustainability, 5*(1), 453.

Ho, T., & Ho, T. (2025). Digital inclusion or exclusion? Exploring the moderating role of governance in digitalization's impact on income inequality in developing countries. *Research in Globalization, 10,* 100283.

International Institute for Environment and Development. (2022, August 25). *Poorest countries at greatest risk of losses and damage from climate change* [Press release]. Retrieved from https://www.iied.org/poorest-countries-greatest-risk-losses-damage-climate-change?utm_source=chatgpt.com

Islam, M. (2024). Rethinking climate justice: Insights from environmental sociology. *Climate, 12*(12), 203.

Jaradat, H., Alshboul, O., Obeidat, I., & Zoubi, M. (2024). Green building, carbon emission, and environmental sustainability of construction industry in Jordan: Awareness, actions and barriers. *Ain Shams Engineering Journal, 15*(2), 102441.

Kamran, M., Raugei, M., & Hutchinson, A. (2023). Critical elements for a successful energy transition: A systematic review. *Renewable and Sustainable Energy Transition, 4,* 100068.

Kapucu, N., Ge, Y., Rott, E., & Isgandar, H. (2024). Urban resilience: Multidimensional perspectives, challenges and prospects for future research. *Urban Governance, 4*(3), 162–179.

Kaygusuz, K. (2016). Hydropower as clean and renewable energy source for electricity generation. *Journal of Engineering Research and Applied Science, 5*(1), 359–369.

Kumar, V., Sharma, K., Kedam, N., Patel, A., Kate, T., & Rathnayake, U. (2024). A comprehensive review on smart and sustainable agriculture using IoT technologies. *Smart Agricultural Technology, 8,* 100487.

Lobato-Peralta, D., Okoye, P., & Alegre, C. (2024). A review on carbon materials for electrochemical energy storage applications: State of the art, implementation, and synergy with metallic compounds for supercapacitor and battery electrodes. *Journal of Power Sources, 617,* 235140.

Mamabolo, E., Mashala, M., Mugari, E., Mogale, T., Mathebula, N., Mabitsela, K., & Ayisi, K. (2025). Application of precision agriculture technologies for crop protection and soil health. *Smart Agricultural Technology, 12,* 101270.

Mamun, A., & Alam, M. (2025). Promoting equity in public health: Addressing inequality and social disparities. *Health Science Reports, 8*(5), e70821.

Mancuso, I., Petruzzelli, A., Panniello, U., & Vaia, G. (2025). The bright and dark sides of AI innovation for sustainable development: Understanding the paradoxical tension between value creation and value destruction. *Technovation, 143,* 103232.

Mangani, P., Khan, G., & Ahmad, N. (2025). Sustainable governance, conflict and environmental justice in critical mineral extraction in Latin America and Africa. *Peace and Sustainability, 1*(3), 100017.

Manisalidis, I., Stavropoulou, E., Stavropoulos, A., & Bezirtzoglou, E. (2020). Environmental and health impacts of air pollution: A review. *Frontiers in Public Health, 8,* 14.

Moya, D., Aldás, C., & Kaparaju, P. (2018). Geothermal energy: Power plant technology and direct heat applications. *Renewable and Sustainable Energy Reviews, 94,* 889–901.

Narayana, T., Venkatesh, C., Kiran, A., Kumar, A., Khan, S., Almusharraf, A., & Quasim, M. (2024). Advances in real time smart monitoring of environmental parameters using IoT and sensors. *Heliyon, 10*(7), e28195.

Nasim, A., Chen, X., al Najjar, B., & Hoang, Y. (2025). The financial sector's response to environmental policy stringency: Comparative analysis of developed and developing economies. *Energy Economics, 144,* 108377.

Nazer, L., Zatarah, R., Waldrip, S., Ke, J., Moukheiber, M., Khanna, A., … Mathur, P. (2023). Bias in artificial intelligence algorithms and recommendations for mitigation. *PLOS Digital Health,* 2(6), e0000278.

Neolaka, Y., Riwu, A., Aigbe, U., Ukhurebor, K., Onyancha, R., Darmokoesoemo, H., & Kusuma, H. (2022). Potential of activated carbon from various sources as a low-cost adsorbent to remove heavy metals and synthetic dyes. *Results in Chemistry, 5,* 100711.

Ngcamu, B. (2023). Climate change effects on vulnerable populations in the global South: A systematic review. *Natural Hazards, 118*(2), 977–991.

Nirmani, P. (2025). Barriers to digital participation in developing countries: Identifying technological, social, and cultural obstacles to community involvement discover the world's research. *GSC Advanced Research and Reviews, 23*(2), 61–71.

Nunes, L. (2023). The rising threat of atmospheric CO2: A review on the causes, impacts, and mitigation strategies. *Environments, 10*(4), 66.

Olawade, D., Wada, O., Ige, A., Egbewole, B., Olojo, A., & Oladapo, B. (2024). Artificial intelligence in environmental monitoring: Advancements, challenges, and future directions. *Hygiene and Environmental Health Advances, 12,* 100114.

Onyancha, R., Aigbe, U., Ukhurebor, K., Kusuma, H., Darmokoesoemo, H., Osibote, O., & Pal, K. (2022). Influence of magnetism-mediated potentialities of recyclable adsorbents for heavy metal ions removal from aqueous solutions – An organized review. *Results in Chemistry, 4,* 100452.

Onyancha, R., Ukhurebor, K., Aigbe, U., Osibote, O., Kusuma, H., Darmokoesoemo, H., & Balogun, V. (2021). A systematic review on the detection and monitoring of toxic gases using carbon nanotube-based biosensors. *Journal of Environmental Management, 330,* 117187.

Osman, A., Chen, L., Yang, M., Msigwa, G., Farghali, M., Fawzy, S., … Yap, P. (2023). Cost, environmental impact, and resilience of renewable energy under a changing climate: A review. *Environmental Chemistry Letters, 21*(2), 741–764.

Panieri, E., Baralic, K., Djukic-Cosic, D., Buha Djordjevic, A., & Saso, L. (2022). PFAS molecules: A major concern for the human health and the environment. *Toxics, 10*(2), 44.

Panja, A., Paul, S., & Jha, P. (2025). Aligning Africa's renewable energy sector with sustainable development goals: Opportunities and challenges. *Sustainable Futures, 9,* 100717.

Papadopoulos, G., Arduini, S., Uyar, H., Psiroukis, V., Kasimati, A., & Fountas, S. (2024). Economic and environmental benefits of digital agricultural technologies in crop production: A review. *Smart Agricultural Technology, 8,* 100441.

Pittri, H., Godawatte, G., Esangbedo, O., Antwi-Afari, P., & Bao, Z. (2025). Exploring barriers to the adoption of digital technologies for circular economy practices in the construction industry in developing countries. *A case of Ghana. Buildings, 15*(7), 1090.

Raman, R. (2017). The impact of genetically modified (GM) crops in modern agriculture: A review. *GM Crops & Food, 8*(4), 195–208.

Resnik, D., & Elliott, K. (2019). Using drones to study human beings: Ethical and regulatory issues. *Science and Engineering Ethics, 25*(3), 707–718.

Rolnick, D., Donti, P., Kaack, L., Kochanski, K., Lacoste, A., Sankaran, K., … Luccioni, A. (2022). Tackling climate change with machine learning. *ACM Computing Surveys (CSUR), 55*(2), 1–96.

Roy, P., Pal, S., Chakrabortty, R., Chowdhuri, I., Saha, A., & Shit, M. (2023). Effects of climate change and sea-level rise on coastal habitat: Vulnerability assessment, adaptation strategies and policy recommendations. *Journal of Environmental Management, 330*, 117187.

Russo, A. (2025). Towards nature-positive smart cities: Bridging the gap between technology and ecology. *Smart Cities, 8*(1), 26.

Sampaio, P., & González, M. (2017). Photovoltaic solar energy: Conceptual framework. *Renewable and Sustainable Energy Reviews, 74*, 590–601.

Sarda, J., Patel, N., Patel, H., Vaghela, R., Brahma, B., Bhoi, A., & Barsocchi, P. (2024). A review of the electric vehicle charging technology, impact on grid integration, policy consequences, challenges and future trends. *Energy Reports, 12*, 5671–5692.

Shen, J., Wang, S., & Wang, Y. (2024). Environmental inequality in peri-urban areas: A case study of Huangpu District, Guangzhou City. *Land, 13*(5), 703.

Shoaib, M., Siddiqui, I., Rehman, S., Khan, S., & Alhems, L. (2019). Assessment of wind energy potential using wind energy conversion system. *Journal of Cleaner Production, 216*, 346–360.

Singh, S., Sarkar, P., & Dutta, K. (2022). Bioenergy: An overview of bioenergy as a sustainable and renewable source of energy. *Bioprospecting of Microbial Diversity*, 483–502. https://doi.org/10.1016/B978-0-323-90958-7.00006-6

Smidt, H., & Jokonya, O. (2022). Factors affecting digital technology adoption by small-scale farmers in agriculture value chains (AVCs) in South Africa. *Information Technology for Development, 28*(3), 558–584.

Sorrell, S., Mallett, A., & Nye, S. (2011). *Barriers to industrial energy efficiency: A literature review.* United Nations Industrial Development Organization (UNIDO).

Summers, H., Stone, T., Dickey, L., Rehmann, C., Zimmerman, E., Tyndall, J., & Liu, L. (2024). Mapping barriers to food, energy, and water systems equity in the United States. *Environmental Science & Policy, 162*, 103941.

Tal, A. (2025). The environmental impacts of overpopulation. *Encyclopedia, 5*(2), 45.

Talaie, A., Kamyab, H., & Razmfarsa, A. (2024). Advancing environmental engineering: The role of artificial intelligence in sustainable solutions-a short review. *Journal of Environmental Treatment Techniques, 12*(3), 14–19.

Tsani, S., Chitou, C., & Overland, I. (2024). Local content policies: Knowledge stock and future directions for research and policy making in view of the sustainability agenda. *Environmental Science & Policy, 162*, 103919.

Ukhurebor, K., Aigbe, U., Onyancha, R., Nwankwo, W., Osibote, O., Paumo, H., … Siloko, I. (2021). Effect of hexavalent chromium on the environment and removal techniques: A review. *Journal of Environmental Management, 280*, 111809.

United Nations (2024). *Global issues: Population.* Retrieved from https://www.un.org/en/global-issues/population#%20:%E2%88%BC:text=The%20world%E2%80%99s%20population%20is%%2020expected,billion%20in%20the%20mid%2D2080s

Venegas, R., Acevedo, J., & Treml, E. (2023). Three decades of ocean warming impacts on marine ecosystems: A review and perspective. *Deep Sea Research Part II: Topical Studies in Oceanography, 212,* 105318.

Wang, Q., Gao, Y., Tang, X., Yang, Z., Tang, L., Luo, G., … Tong, H.. (2025). How aging microplastics influence heavy metal environmental fate and bioavailability: A systematic review. *Environmental Research, 271,* 121128.

Waqas, M., Naseem, A., Humphries, U., Hlaing, P., Shoaib, M., & Hashim, S. (2025). A comprehensive review of the impacts of climate change on agriculture in Thailand. *Farming System, 3*(1), 100114.

Watson, R., Baste, I., Larigauderie, A., Leadley, P., Pascual, U., Baptiste, B., … Fischer, M.. (2019). *Summary for policymakers of the global assessment report on biodiversity and ecosystem services of the Intergovernmental Science-Policy Platform on Biodiversity and Ecosystem Services.* Bonn, Germany: IPBES Secretariat, 22–47.

Wiens, J. (2016). Climate-related local extinctions are already widespread among plant and animal species. *PLoS Biology, 14*(12), e2001104.

World Bank Group (n.d.). *Climate Change Threatens to Deepen Poverty in East Asia Pacific by 2030.* Retrieved from https://www.worldbank.org/en/news/press-release/2015/11/12/climate-change-threatens-to-deepen-poverty-in-east-asia-pacific-by-2030?utm_source=chatgpt.com

Yazici, İ, Shayea, I., & Din, J. (2023). A survey of applications of artificial intelligence and machine learning in future mobile networks-enabled systems. *Engineering Science and Technology, an International Journal, 44,* 101455.

Zhu, M., Wang, J., Yang, X., Zhang, Y., Zhang, L., Ren, H., … Ye, L. (2022). A review of the application of machine learning in water quality evaluation. *Eco-Environment & Health, 1*(2), 107–116.

2

Machine Learning Fundamentals for Environmental Monitoring and Remediation

Abstract

The integration of machine learning (ML) into environmental monitoring and remediation has revolutionized the entire field of environmental science through improved data analysis mechanisms, automation of reporting, and enhanced monitoring and remediation strategies. Consequently, it offers better quality in communication at stakeholder levels, which has resulted in timely and improved decision-making and accelerated policy formulation. It is important to note that ML has been extensively employed in many environmental applications, such as air, water, and soil quality monitoring, biodiversity conservation, and tracking and analyzing climate change due to enhanced data processing speed and the level of accuracy inherent in data modelling. In comparison to conventional techniques, ML is efficient, time-saving, highly accurate, scalable, adaptive, cost-effective, easy to integrate with data, and has a lower long-term maintenance cost, hence its rapid rise and usage in environmental science. Therefore, this chapter covers the fundamentals of ML for environmental monitoring and remediation through the sections that are segmented as introduction, fundamentals of ML, classes of ML, core ML algorithms and their environmental relevance, evaluation metrics in machine learning, applications of ML in monitoring and remediation, and conclusion and future recommendations.

2.1 Introduction

In recent years, the world has experienced rapid population growth, accelerated industrialization, and a surge in urbanization, all of which have significantly exerted pressure on the environment, resulting in continuous degradation and pollution. Therefore, there is an urgent global demand to collectively collaborate on addressing the rising deterioration of air quality, climate instability, water contamination, and soil degradation (Nguyen, Grote, Neubacher, Do, & Paudel, 2023). In that regard, and over time, monitoring

DOI: 10.1201/9781003618584-2

and mitigation efforts have been employed to address these challenges. The monitoring process entails carefully observing, measuring, and analyzing environmental conditions to identify changes that could harm ecosystems (Olawade et al., 2024). It is important to note that environmental monitoring intends to identify baseline parameters, the temporal trends, and recognize emerging issues that can be used to formulate and tailor policies for management interventions (Figure 2.1) (Kumar et al., 2021).

Traditional methods of monitoring the environment that have been employed across different periods involve using data records, running lab tests, and collecting samples by hand (Kumar et al., 2021). Despite these conventional methods being useful, they are inherently costly, time-consuming, use manual sampling, are localized measurements, and suffer from accuracy issues. The challenge of finding skilled personnel, coupled with the lack of sophisticated and modern equipment in developing countries, has equally contributed to the limited establishment of environmental monitoring initiatives (Afoma et al., 2025). Consequently, this has hindered many countries and regions from conducting regular and large-scale monitoring and forecasting activities, leading to weakened efforts in dealing with environmental challenges (Li, Feng, Chen, Zhao, & Wang, 2020). Also, lengthy delays in obtaining results only obstruct prompt decision-making in situations that need swift action in attempts to avert environmental damage or reduce threats to public health (Olawade et al., 2024).

In this context, advanced technologies that address the limitations of the conventional methods have been sought and employed. For instance, the

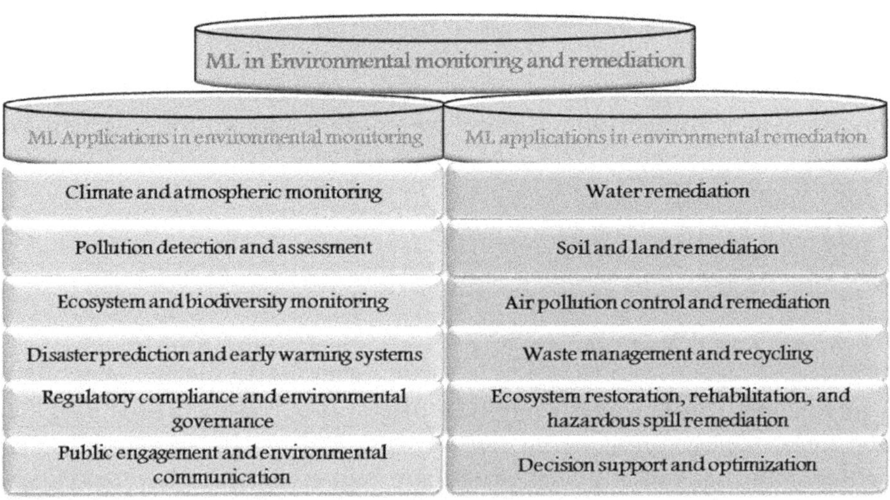

FIGURE 2.1
Applications of ML in environmental monitoring and remediation. (From Kumar et al. (2021), licensed under the CC BY 4.0 license.) (http://creativecommons.org/licenses/by/4.0/)

introduction of sensor-based monitoring networks, remote sensing technologies, and the Internet of Things (IoT) has emerged as exciting strategies to provide continuous, real-time data streams and facilitate widespread environmental data collection for practical monitoring, analysis, and decision-making (Mishra, 2025).

A combination of the above technologies with machine learning (ML) produces systems that are superior and intelligent, capable of monitoring, detecting, and predicting environmental phenomena. The working mechanism of ML is to learn from the specific data given, identify patterns, and make predictions. These present ML as an advanced tool in all fields that are data-driven (Soori, Arezoo, & Dastres, 2023).

ML enables the integration of large and multi-dimensional datasets containing environmental parameters that are collected from satellites, remote sensors, labs, and IoT systems. Then the algorithms identify patterns, understand the relationships, and predict environmental phenomena with a higher degree of accuracy and scalability when compared to traditional statistical methods (Essamlali, Nhaila, & El Khaili, 2024). Furthermore, emerging technologies such as big data analytics, cloud computing, and digital twins have intensified and revolutionized environmental management by offering platforms that replicate physical objects, systems, or real-time data to accurately reflect the characteristics of their real-world counterparts (Attaran & Celik, 2023).

Notably, the use of ML to address environmental and ecological phenomena is well documented. For example, an Artificial Neural Network (ANN) and Adaptive Neuro-Fuzzy Inference System (ANFIS) have been used to predict the monthly rainfall, thus helping meteorological stations to predict weather and aid in planning (Abebe & Endalie, 2023). Similarly, ANN random forest (RF) models were employed to determine the earthquake depth, acceleration, and velocity accuracy aimed at guiding planning during natural disasters, with ANN found to give better results (Essam, Kumar, Ahmed, Murti, & El-Shafie, 2021). Furthermore, Castelli, Clemente, Popovič, Silva, & Vanneschi (2020) conducted a study on the use of support vector regression (SVR) to evaluate the pollutant and particle levels, where an accuracy prediction of 94.1% of CO, O_3, and SO_2 pollutants was reported. Also, Panigrahi et al. (2023) have used SVR and logistic regression to predict the quality of drinking water, where prediction accuracies of 98% and 92% were determined, respectively. Equally, a multi-layer perception neural network (MLP-NN) model has been accurately used to predict the changes in water levels, which has since helped in planning during flooding periods (Zakaria, Malek, Zolkepli, & Ahmed, 2021). Classification and Regression Tree (CART) has been employed to examine the factors influencing forest fire, with the study showing that the slope as a factor substantially influenced forest fires (Piao, Lee, Park, Kim, & Jin, 2022). In the circular economy, ANN has been used to study the projection of flue gas from waste to energy. The findings, which showed an RME of 0.03 and 0.19, were used to decide on renewable energy (Ma et al., 2022).

The establishment and integration of ML systems have provided holistic frameworks aimed at ensuring sustainable resource utilization, guidance on best practices in the circular economy, and protecting the ecosystems. These explain why governments, research institutions, and other industry players are increasingly employing and adopting ML platforms based on environmental intelligence to help formulate policies, evaluate impact assessments, and monitor compliance (Jose, Panigrahi, Patil, Fernando, & Ramakrishna, 2020; Velenturf & Purnell, 2021).

In view of the aforementioned, this chapter provides an all-inclusive summary of the fundamentals of ML in environmental monitoring. The organization of the chapter begins with the introduction, which covers the need and integration of ML into environmental monitoring and remediation as an advanced technology, followed by the fundamentals of ML (core concepts, types of ML learning, common algorithms, and model evaluation metrics). This is then followed by examples of applications of ML in environmental monitoring and remediation, advanced computational techniques, and challenges, as well as future directions.

2.2 Fundamentals of Machine Learning

The emergence of ML as a realm in AI has provided a new pathway through which data-driven insights and decision-making are derived and applied across many fields, where environmental monitoring and remediation is one of them (Stephen, 2024). The evolution of AI started in the early 1950s when systems were crafted on a rule-based approach in the academic discipline to aid in decision-making. In the 1980s, the ML was developed mainly for optimization, where algorithms were allowed to learn patterns in the datasets and predict the outcome. Thereafter, in the 2010s, deep learning (DL) was designed, and it consisted of input, hidden, and output layers whose functionality mirrors that of the human brain (Figure 2.2) (Janga, Reddy, & Raviteja, 2023).

It is essential to note that traditional statistical approaches to environmental models are based on empirical relationships derived from physical or chemical equations, which are often straightforward to solve using linear systems. However, environmental systems are nonlinear, very dynamic, and more often influenced by many interacting variables/parameters, which are difficult to quantify and solve explicitly (Pianosi et al., 2016). These shortcomings of traditional approaches can be easily addressed by employing ML, as it is flexible and adaptive to different data structures, allowing it to identify complex patterns and relationships without the need for conventional formulations (Umutoni & Samadi, 2024).

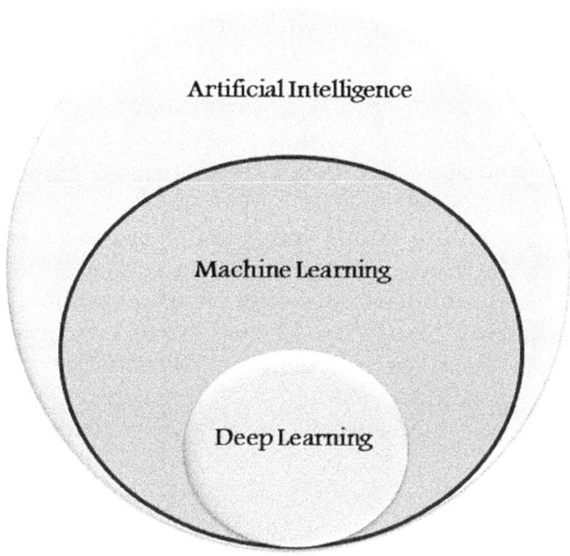

FIGURE 2.2
Artificial Intelligence, Machine Learning, and Deep Learning. (From Janga et al., (2023), Elsevier. With Permission.)

In mathematical form, an ML model tries to approximate an unknown function (improve performance through experience) $f: X \rightarrow Y$. Here, the X are the input parameters or variables and Y, the output or target variable. As an example, in determining the efficiency of heavy metal or dye removal from wastewater, factors such as pH, temperature, heavy metal/dye concentration, and contact time are used as input variables (independent variables) (Janga et al., 2023). In contrast, the removal efficiency is the target or dependent variable. The objective of the ML model is to minimize the error or the loss function, L(y, ŷ) (Equation 2.1).

$$L(\theta) = \frac{1}{N} \sum_{i=1}^{N} L(y_i, f_\theta(x_i)) \tag{2.1}$$

Here the N, x_i, y_i, $f_\theta(x_i)$ and $L(y_i, f_\theta(x_i))$ are the number of training samples, input for the sample i, output, model prediction, and the loss function measuring prediction error, respectively.

When compared to the conventional statistical regression, where they are defined by a specific functional form, ML models have no predefined functional form. Instead, it learns directly from the datasets through a series of iterative training and optimization using various functionalities like gradient descent (Janga et al., 2023).

2.3 Classes of Machine Learning

2.3.1 Supervised Learning

This type of learning involves training models on labelled datasets. Here, the input features (variables) and target outputs are all known. The objective of this class is for the models to learn a mapping function that can precisely generalise the unseen data. This type of learning has two types, namely, regression, where the output is continuous, and classification, which has a discrete output. The commonly used supervised algorithms include simple regression, multivariate regression, support vector machines, random forests, decision trees, lasso regression, Naïve Bayes, logistic regression, and K-Nearest Neighbours. These models learn from the examples given during the training period and generalize to new occurrences (Cipriano, Noce, Mereu, & Santini, 2025).

2.3.2 Unsupervised Learning

Unlike supervised learning, here the data is unlabeled, and models are used to analyse to uncover hidden structures, clusters, or patterns. The models are quite instrumental in exploratory data analysis and dimensionality reduction. They can broadly be grouped into three main categories, namely, (1) clustering algorithms such as k-means clustering, hierarchical clustering, DBSCAN, mean-shift clustering, spectral clustering, principal component analysis (PCA), and independent component analysis (ICA), which are designed to group similar data points (2) association algorithms like apriori algorithm and frequent pattern growth which can explicitly identify relationships and frequent patterns among data items and (3) anomaly detection algorithms which includes isolation forest and Z-score algorithm which are capable of finding unusual observations that do not fit or conform to the general data pattern (Cipriano et al., 2025).

2.3.3 Reinforcement Learning

This type of learning involves sequential decision-making problems, where an agent interacts with the environment to achieve a specific goal. Upon the interactions and based on the actions, there are rewards earned or penalties given, which accumulate over a given period of time. There are three different types of reinforcement algorithms. The first one is the value-based strategies, such as Q-Learning, Deep Q-Networks, and SARSA, which are meant to learn the value of actions in different states. The second one is the policy-based methods, such as REINFORCE and Proximal Policy Optimization, that are designed to directly focus on optimizing the action selection policy. Lastly, there are the actor-critic algorithms, which include the Advantage

Actor-Critic (A2C), Asynchronous Advantage Actor-Critic (A3C), and Soft Actor-Critic (SAC), that are capable of combining both the value- and policy-based techniques for improved stability and performance (Cipriano et al., 2025).

2.4 Workflow of Machine Learning

The typical ML workflow for environmental monitoring and remediation consists of eight main sequential steps, which include data acquisition, data preprocessing, feature engineering, model selection, model training, model validation and testing, deployment and feedback, and continuous improvement (Figure 2.3).

For environmental monitoring and remediation, data are collected from sources that include laboratory analyses, remote sensing, and open databases that handle environmental parameters like the NASA EarthData database. Sequentially, upon collection, these data then undergo cleaning, normalization, imputation, and feature engineering processes depending on the model specifications or general analytical functions (Sang, Xu, & de Vrieze, 2021). This stage is fundamentally important because more often than not, environmental datasets contain missing values or suffer from irregular sampling intervals. Feature engineering involves feature selection and feature extraction, which rely heavily on domain knowledge and experience to determine relevant features (Mohammadi et al., 2019). The next phase involves the selection of the model and training, which occurs through the appropriate selection of an ideal ML algorithm corresponding to the problem type, the objectives of the research, data types (structured or unstructured), scale, and distributions (Hao et al., 2025).

The identified model is then iteratively trained on the training dataset by adjusting parameters and hyperparameters to establish a mapping between features and labels (Kooh, Lim, Lim, & Malik, 2019). Then, model optimization

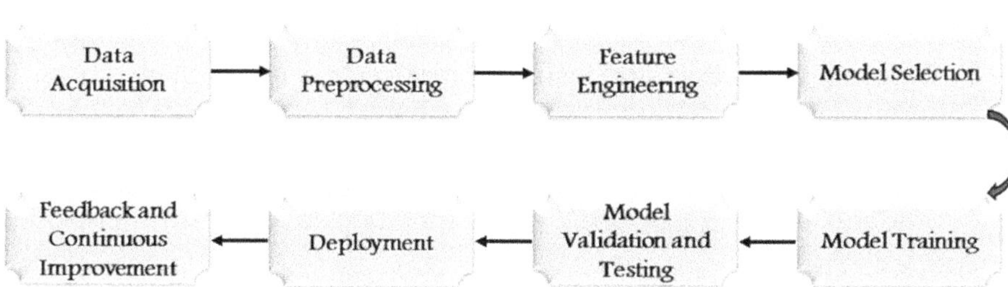

FIGURE 2.3
A representation of the eight sequential stages of the ML workflow.

algorithms like the stochastic gradient descent and Adam are used to minimize the loss functions. The trained models are then subsequently, model evaluation and validation are required after training to quantify the model's performance and robustness, respectively. Performance metrics, such as RMSE, MAE, R^2, accuracy, precision, recall, and F1-score, among others, as listed in Table 2.1, are employed in this process. In case of performance limitations, a revision of the model network structure coupled with fine-tuning its parameters, applying data augmentation techniques, or implementing ensemble learning approaches is used (Zhao et al., 2023).

Deployment and interpretation of the trained model provide access to real-time prediction and guide decision-making through visualization tools and AI tools, such as SHAP and LIME, helping environmental managers draw insights from various occurrences. The last stage of the ML workflow involves the integration of the feedback mechanisms that are aimed at improving and optimizing the developed ML systems.

2.5 Fundamentals of Machine Learning

2.5.1 Key Concepts in Machine Learning

The concepts in ML are diverse and generally apply to all ML systems or processes. Here we will discuss concepts such as features and labels, training, validation, and testing, overfitting and underfitting, and model generalization.

1. **Features and Labels:** Features represent independent measurable parameters (variables) or characteristics that are fed into the model, whereas labels or outputs are the targeted variable or quantity that is predicted. For example, Figure 2.4, which shows a representation to determine the removal efficiency in the adsorption of methylene blue (MB) using ML, initial MB concentration, pH, sorbent dose, and time are the features (Aigbe et al., 2025b). The desired prediction, which is more often called the dependent variable (outcome), is the percentage removal of MB, hence the label.
2. **Training, validation, and testing:** Are subsets of data obtained from the available data to fit the model parameters, tune hyperparameters (prevent overfitting), and evaluate final model performance, respectively. The dataset is typically subdivided into 70% training, 15% validation, and 15% testing (Montesinos López, Montesinos López, & Crossa, 2022).
3. **Overfitting and underfitting:** Overfitting arises when the model learns on noise as opposed to learning and identifying the true underlying pattern, thereby leading to generalization of the

TABLE 2.1

Regression and Classification Metrics in Machine Learning Model Evaluation

Metrics	Formula	Definition of Terms	Significance
Coefficient of Determination	$R^2 = 1 - \frac{\sum_{i=1}^{n}\left(y_i - \widehat{y}_i\right)^2}{\sum_{i=1}^{n}\left(y_i - \bar{y}\right)^2}$	y_i, $\widehat{y}_i$, and $\bar{y}$ are the actual, predicted, and mean values	When $R^2 = 1$, it implies perfect prediction, while $R^2 = 0$ shows that the model does no better than the mean of the data
Root Mean Square Error	$RMSE = \sqrt{\frac{1}{n}\sum_{i=1}^{n}\left(y_i - \widehat{y}_i\right)^2}$	y_i *and* $\widehat{y}_i$ are the actual and predicted values	It is useful for detecting outliers or misprediction since it is sensitive to large deviations. Lower RMSE shows higher model precision
Mean Absolute Error	$MAE = \frac{1}{n}\sum_{i=1}^{n}\left\lvert y_i - \widehat{y}_i\right\rvert$	y_i *and* $\widehat{y}_i$ are the actual and predicted values	MAE is more robust than RMSE on outliers and offers easy prediction of errors
Mean Absolute Percentage Error	$MAPE = \frac{100}{n}\sum_{i=1}^{n}\left\lvert\frac{y_i - \widehat{y}_i}{y_i}\right\rvert$	y_i *and* $\widehat{y}_i$ are the actual and predicted values	More useful for comparing model performance in different datasets
Nash–Sutcliffe Efficiency	$NSE = 1 - \frac{\Sigma\left(y_i - \widehat{y}_i\right)^2}{\Sigma\left(y_i - \bar{y}\right)^2}$	y_i, $\widehat{y}_i$ and $\bar{y}$ are the actual, predicted, and mean values	It is similar to R^2, but it is more sensitive to the differences between predicted and observed temporal patterns For NSE > 0.8, it generally shows a good model performance
Precision	$\frac{TP}{TP + FP}$	TP is a true positive, and FP false positive	It is suitable when the goal is to minimize false positives
Recall	$\frac{TP}{TP + FN}$	TP is a true positive, and FP false positive	It is used to measure the ability of the model to identify positive classes. Ideal in cases that missed detections
F1	$\frac{2 \times precision \times recall}{Precision + recall}$		Suitable for imbalanced categories or the demand to balance both the false positives and negatives
Accuracy	$\frac{TP + TN}{TP + FP + TN + FN}$	TP is a true positive, FN is, false negative, and FP false positive	Ideal for category-balanced data, but might be misleading when dealing with imbalanced data

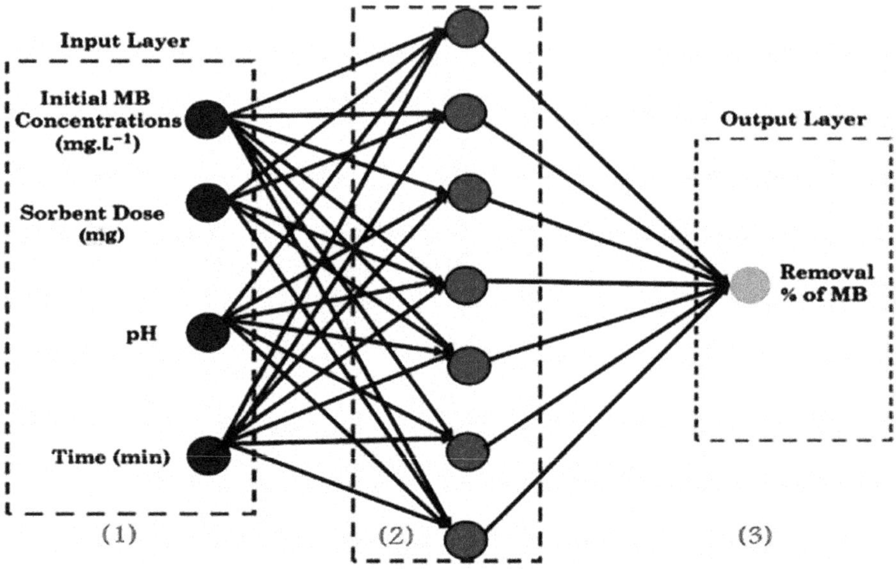

FIGURE 2.4
A schematic representation of the deep learning process for methylene blue dye removal. (From Aigbe et al. (2025b), Elsevier. With Permission.)

model. On the other hand, when the model is too simple to learn and capture the data complexity, it results in underfitting. These two occurrences can be mitigated through techniques such as cross-validation, regularization, and dropout in neural networks (Aliferis & Simon, 2024). Overfitting and underfitting are primarily caused by limited data volume and a poor fit between the model's complexity and the dataset's characteristics (Hao et al., 2025).

4. **Model generalization**: Model generalization is basically the ability of a model to predict or forecast on unseen data correctly. In environmental science, various strategies such as transfer learning and domain adaptation have been formulated to improve cross-regional generalization. (Wang et al., 2025).

2.5.2 Core ML Algorithms and Their Environmental Relevance

2.5.2.1 Linear Regression

This is one of the simplest ML models that draws a linear relationship between an independent variable/target x and a dependent variable y, as represented in Equation 2.2.

$$y = \beta_0 + \beta_1 x + \epsilon \tag{2.2}$$

The terms β_0 and β_1 are coefficients, whereas ϵ is the error term. This model is characterized by low computational demand and easy interpretability, thereby making it ideal for preliminary environmental analysis despite its simplicity. It has been widely used in modelling the concentration of air pollutants (Kazi, Filip, & Kazi, 2023; Ndiaye et al., 2024), groundwater contaminants (Banerjee, Ó'Domhnaill, Creedon, Jones, & Gharbia, 2025), and temperature variations/trends (Parlak & Yavaşoğlu, 2023). Conversely, for nonlinear relationships, their performance has always been poor (Messaoud et al., 2020).

2.5.2.2 Decision Trees

Decision trees (DTs) are another very predominant model used in environmental data, where they work by recursively splitting a dataset into smaller subsets based on the values of input features or variables. It is basically designed as a tree, where it is comprised of several decisions and the possible and potential outcomes (Gunasekaran, Sreevardhan, & SamiKannu, 2025). Importantly, each internal node of this model represents a decision rule, while each leaf node corresponds to a final predicted outcome.

Equation 2.3 represents the decision tree classifier:

$$H(x) = argmax\left(\Sigma_{t=1}^{T}\left[y_i = c\right]p(iIx)\right) \quad (2.3)$$

where $H(x)$ represents the predicted class whose inputs as x, the c is the class label, y_i is the training instance (i-th), N is the number of training samples, and $p(iIx)$ is the probability of an instance i given x (Gunasekaran et al., 2025).

The DTs are simple, easy to train, and interpretable, hence ideal to model environmental parameters influencing pollution (Özüpak, Alpsalaz, & Aslan, 2025) or the remediation process. However, they are affected by overfitting, particularly when dealing with noisy and complex data, coupled with occasionally not performing well on learning tasks that involve image recognition or natural language processing (NLP) (Olawade et al., 2024).

2.5.2.3 Random Forests (RF)

The RFs build on DTs by constructing an ensemble (array) of multiple trees that are trained randomly on different subsets of data. Through classification or regression, the output of these ensembles is aggregated to determine the outcome, which aids in reducing overfitting, enhancing generalization (since each tree works on a distinct subset of data), and improving precision (Gunasekaran et al., 2025). The RF classifier is represented by Equation 2.4.

$$y = mode\{f1(x), f2(x), f3(x), \ldots\ldots\ldots, fn(x)\} \quad (2.4)$$

where y is the final predicted label, $f1(x)$ is the predicted class label and n is the number of all DT in a forest (Gunasekaran et al., 2025).

RFs are designed to accommodate different data types like images and texts (Abu El-Magd, Soliman, Morsy, & Kharbish, 2023). They are particularly used in environmental monitoring tasks like image classification, time series prediction, and natural language processing (Olawade et al., 2024).

2.5.2.4 Gradient Boosting Machines (GBMs) and XGBoost

Models like GBMs and XGBoost sequentially train trees, leading to the minimization and correction of errors, thereby enhancing predictive performance. It operates by gradually involving new DT into the model, and every tree is now trained to correct the errors and mistakes made by the previous tree. By summing up all the projections made for the trees, a prediction or forecast is determined. The GBM classifier is mathematically represented in Equation 2.5.

$$F(x) = \sum_{m=1}^{M} \eta(x) H_m(x) \tag{2.5}$$

where $F(x)$ is the prediction, η is the learning rate, M total number of trees, and $H_m(x)$ is the prediction of the Mth decision tree (Gunasekaran et al., 2025).

They are computationally efficient and provide high accuracy in applications such as predicting PM2.5 levels (Wang, Wu, & Wu, 2023) and adsorption kinematics optimizations (Hassan & Kazemi, 2025). Importantly, XGBoost has gained attention in the preprocessing stage of the ML workflow due to its speed and ability to deal with missing data (Jinbo, Yufu, & Haitao, 2025).

2.5.2.5 Support Vector Machines (SVMs)

These models are suitable for dealing with highly dimensional data, providing insights by learning complex relationships in dataset parameters, and are applicable across different types of data (Manikandan & Abirami, 2021). It is capable of performing tasks of both binary and multi-classification due to its unique effectiveness. It works on the premise of identifying the hyperplane that fully separates the data points into definite classes while maintaining the focus on maximizing the margin between the hyperplane and the nearest data points (Gunasekaran et al., 2025). The equation of the SVM algorithm can be expressed as Equation 2.6.

$$y(x) = sgm(wT \times x + b) \tag{2.6}$$

where $y(x), w,\ T,$ and b are the predicted label from the feature x, the weight vector and b is the bias term that shifts the hyperplane away from the origin.

The SVMs are applicable in deforestation and recognizing wildlife through a classification process (Zagajewski et al., 2021), extracting information from environmental reports through NLP (Meza, Yepes, Rodrigo-Ilarri, & Cassiraga, 2019), and are also used in regression tasks to forecast environmental parameters (Ye et al., 2020). The SVR model has also shown excellent results when modelling and predicting HM adsorption efficiency (Parveen, Zaidi, & Danish, 2019), water quality indices (Mohd Zebaral Hoque, Ab. Aziz, Alelyani, Mohana, & Hosain, 2022), and soil organic carbon estimation (Song et al., 2022).

2.5.2.6 *Artificial Neural Networks (ANNs)*

The ANNs are designed to mimic the human brain's neural architecture through hierarchical layers of interconnected neurons that are responsible for processing and transmitting signals (Lakra et al., 2025). The feedforward architecture consists of an input layer, a hidden layer, and an output layer, with each neuron providing a weighted summation that is then followed by an activation function (Gunasekaran et al., 2025). Notably, the input is fed to each neuron, which processes it through the weighted sums and an activation function that is non-linear, hence allowing the system to identify and capture underlying data patterns from the input, as shown in Equation 2.7.

$$y = f(W.x + b) \tag{2.7}$$

In Equation 2.7, x is the input features, b is the bias vector, and W is the weight matrix.

2.5.2.7 *Convolutional Neural Networks (CNNs)*

In environmental data, CNNs are designed to process spatial data by applying filters to extract hierarchical spatial features, making these models particularly suitable for remote sensing and satellite imagery analysis. The fact that they can learn complex configurations without traditional programming makes them suitable for applications like land-use and land-cover mapping (Hosseiny et al., 2023), detection of flood and drought (Noori, Ziboon, & AL-Hameedawi, 2025.; Goyal, 2024), and the detection of deforestation and the expansion of urban areas (Javed, Kim, Lee, Oh, & Han, 2023).

2.5.2.8 *Recurrent Neural Networks (RNNs) and Long Short-Term Memory (LSTM)*

The RNN models are specifically devised to process sequential data and effectively predict time-series phenomena. To enable long-term temporal learning, LSTRM introduces a gating mechanism that is meant to address the vanishing gradient challenges, hence effective in forecasting extreme weather occurrences and retrieving information from environmental reports (Niroomand, Pahlavani, Bigdeli, & Ghorbanzadeh, 2025). The examples where the RNN and LSTM have been applied include forecasting air pollutant levels (Belavadi, Rajagopal, & Mohan, 2020), predicting hydrological flow (Ley, Bormann, & Casper, 2023), and monitoring biogas production (Pino Santana, Garcia-Gen, Dewasme, & Vande Wouwer, 2025). Importantly, a combination of LTSM-based models with external data like meteorological parameters has been found to outperform traditional autoregressive models such as ARIMA and SARIMA in modelling and predicting temporal environmental data (Hossain, Shams, & Ullah, 2025). Nevertheless, they require large datasets and are expensive to computationally model.

2.5.2.9 Hybrid and Ensemble Deep Learning Models

The integration of CNN and LSTM to form hybrid architectures has ensured that both spatial and temporal dependencies available in environmental datasets are captured. This has shown the hybrid models applied in the spatio-temporal mapping of pollution (Chen, Chen, Li, & Chen, 2025) and dynamic ecosystem modelling (Sinha et al., 2025) with high accuracy achieved. Apart from hybrid architectures, ensemble models, which combine traditional algorithms like RF with deep learning, such as LSTM, to form RF-LSTM, have shown enhanced robustness due to the synergic effect of many complementary strengths of the models involved (Wali, Khan, Zhang, & Shakoor, 2025). Both hybrid and ensemble DL models are fundamentally important in capturing the complexity of features and labels of complex and nonlinear environmental parameters. While they can be complex and expensive to train and provide interpretation, they offer better performance (Olawade et al., 2024).

2.6 Evaluation Metrics in Machine Learning

Evaluation metrics have been developed to provide to standardize how models are evaluated. Different kinds of metrics have been designed to perform distinct tasks (regression or classification), thereby showing model performance. Table 2.1 shows the widely used metrics for regression, which include Coefficient of Determination (R^2), Root Mean Square Error (RMSE), Mean Absolute Error (MAE), Mean Absolute Percentage Error (MAPE), and Nash–Sutcliffe Efficiency (NSE), and classification metrics like Precision, Recall, F1-score, and Accuracy (Hao et al., 2025).

2.7 Data Mining and Preprocessing for Environmental Systems

2.7.1 Data Mining

To effectively and reliably conduct environmental monitoring and remediation, it is critical to ensure that the data is of high quality, the right quantity, and representative. Imperatively, the effectiveness of ML models is dependent on the integrity of the input data. The environmental data is fundamentally heterogeneous since it is obtained from ground-based sensors, remote sensing satellites, laboratories, and through simulations. The collection of data through ground-based sensor networks has revolutionized environmental research, since the data acquired is of high quality and real-time (Figure 2.5). Fundamental parameters on air pollutants, water quality, and soil nutrients can be traced through smart sensor grids (Dharmarathne, Abekoon, Bogahawaththa, Alawatugoda, & Meddage, 2025). Ground-based observations have been complemented by using satellite-based sensors such as Landsat and Sentinel in the remote sensing field to provide large-scale and long-term data. They have been effectively used in monitoring land use, climate change, and in estimating chlorophyll and turbidity in aquatic systems (Majid, Ikhsan, & Hassan, 2025).

Controlled laboratory research offers high-quality data needed for modelling and simulating environmental phenomena. Despite their small volumes, studies on research areas such as adsorption, photocatalysis, and bioremediation generate data on crucial parameters that can be used to train regression or ANN-based models (Aigbe et al., 2025b; Aigbe et al., 2025a). Similarly, open-access databases and citizen science platforms such as AirNow, NOAA

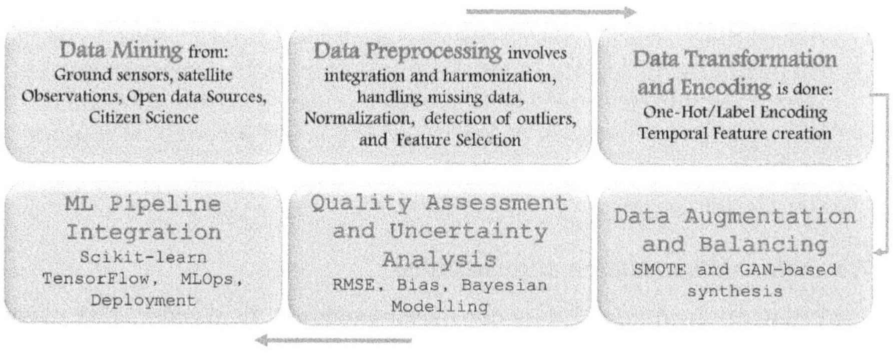

FIGURE 2.5
A schematic representation of the preprocessing procedure of environmental data for ML modelling.

Climate Data Store, and Copernicus Open Access Hub are now available and provide expanded access to diverse environmental data for ML projects (Rosales et al., 2025).

Data obtained from these methods has diverse challenges, which include missing values, different resolutions, formats, scales, calibration errors, environmental fluctuations from sensors, and high dimensionality; hence, there is a need to mitigate these challenges to ensure data reliability, improved model performance, and interpretability are achieved (Sierra-Porta, 2024).

2.7.2 Data Preprocessing

Data preprocessing is a crucial phase in ML as it transforms raw data into an acceptable standard for ML models. The steps involved in preprocessing are outlined as follows (Koukaras & Tjortjis, 2025):

- The fact that environmental data is obtained from multiple sources, there is often a need for harmonization to ensure the attainment of spatial resolution, reference in coordinate systems, and temporal frequency.
- Consequently, handling of missing data through deletion methods for small proportions of missing data, imputation through mean/median, k-nearest neighbour, multiple imputation, and the use of ML algorithms like RF to predict missing values.
- To improve data stability, noise filtering is very important and can be done through statistical filters, such as Z-score and IQR, to detect anomalies or through ML methods.
- Data is then rescaled to ensure feature compatibility through Min-Max normalization, which transforms values to the [0,1] range, and through Z-score standardization by using the mean and standard deviation.
- Then, finally, to reduce overfitting and ensure an enhancement of interpretability, feature selection is performed by using filter methods, embedded methods (LASSO and DTs), and through laWrapper methods.

2.7.3 Data Transformation and Encoding

More often, environmental data consist of categorical variables. The use of encoding methods such as One-Hot encoding (which creates binary vectors of each category), Label encoding (gives numerical values to categorical variables), and Target Encoding (which uses target-related statistics to replace categorical data) are used to transform these variables (Koukaras & Tjortjis, 2025; Maharana, Mondal, & Nemade, 2022).

2.7.4 Data Augmentation and Balancing

This step is fundamentally important when datasets are small or imbalanced. Two techniques, namely the Synthetic Minority Over-sampling Technique (SMOTE) and Generative Adversarial Networks (GANs), are employed to balance classification datasets and to synthetically create more environmental data samples, respectively (Koukaras & Tjortjis, 2025; Maharana et al., 2022).

2.7.5 Data Quality Assessment

Data quality and assessment are done to ensure the ML models' forecasting and prediction are trustworthy. Important statistical measures like RMSE and R^2, as shown in Table 2.2, are used together with uncertainty propagation techniques to evaluate the reliability of data. In environmental datasets, Bayesian frameworks have progressively been used to quantify uncertainty (Koukaras & Tjortjis, 2025; Maharana et al., 2022).

2.8 Integration of Data Preprocessing in ML Pipelines

Modern ML platforms have functionalities for integrating various preprocessing workflows into automated pipelines, such as Scikit-learn Pipelines and TensorFlow Data Validation, which are meant for data cleaning automation and scaling. Also, MLOps frameworks have been used to ensure consistency is achieved between training and deployment environments (Koukaras & Tjortjis, 2025; Maharana et al., 2022).

2.9 Applications in Environmental Monitoring and Remediation

The use of ML in environmental monitoring and remediation is widely reported, and it serves as a foundational tool in ensuring a proper, sustainable management of natural resources is attained and aiding in the detection and mitigation of environmental degradation. As shown in Table 2.2, ML has been employed in the study of water quality monitoring and detection of contamination, specifically in predicting and mapping nitrate in

TABLE 2.2

Applications of Machine Learning in Various Environmental Settings.

Research Purpose	Location	Model	Source of Data	Results	Metrics	Recommendations	References
Predict groundwater nitrate susceptibility for targeting interventions	Water Quality Monitoring and Contamination Detection	ANN, CART, RF, and SVM	Field-measured data and existing GIS hydrogeological data	RF and SVM models could be used to identify areas at high risk of nitrate contamination using spatial variability, GIS-aided visualization, and easily accessible field-measured groundwater quality data	RF (R^2: 0.74; RMSE: 3.5) and SVM (R^2: 0.80; RMSE: 2.8)	Use RF with explainability (feature importance / SHAP) and include easily measured hydrochemical predictors for local management.	(Lee et al., 2023)
Predict biogas production / optimize anaerobic digestion	Bioremediation	Artificial Neural Network (ANN / MLP)	Operational digester data (feedstock composition, temp, pH, retention time)	ANN provided accurate biogas-yield forecasts and captured nonlinear relationships better than simple kinetic models	$R^2 = 0.54–0.76$	Adopt ANN-based forecasting for real-time digester control and co-digestion optimization	(Guo et al., 2024)
Prediction of air quality	Air Quality Monitoring and Prediction	CNN-RNN hybrid	Experimental	The CNN-RNN hybrid offered high accuracy in the prediction of PM2.5	MAE =1.620 R2 = 0.995 Milan MAE = 2.511 R2 = 0.834 MAE = 0.516 R2 = 0.995	Provide an effective way of predicting PM2.5 concentrations	(Utku et al., 2025)

Air quality index and prediction of pollutant and particle levels	Air Quality Monitoring and Prediction	SVR	Environmental and Protection Agency (USA)	Accuracy rate of 94.1% in modelling for O_3, CO_3, and SO_2 pollutants	R2 = 0.941	Need to improve SVR use in prediction and compare with other ML models	(Castelli et al., 2020)
Groundwater nitrate mapping	Water Quality Monitoring and Contamination Detection	GB, RF, XG, and AD	Experimental	GB outperformed other models	GB metrics R2 = 0.627, MAE = 0.529, RMSE = 0.705, PICP = 0.924	The study recommends the use of ML spatial prediction for nitrate pollution in groundwater	(Liang, et al., 2024)
Heavy metals evaluation in soils	Adsorption	RF	Experimental	Unlike Cd, Pb, As, and Hg, Cr and Ni are less affected by human activities.	R2 = 0.63	To map a more spatial distribution of HMs, the inclusion of more environmental factors and different prediction techniques is recommended	(Nie, Chen, Sun, & An, 2024)
Prediction of Methylene blue dye adsorption	Adsorption	ANN and ANFIS	Experimental	Potential of RSM, ANN, and ANFIS in dye removal	ANN (R2 = 0.8864), and ANFIS (R2 = 0.9589)	Study recommends use of Oryza sativa straw biomass adsorbent for methylene blue dye removal	(Kumari et al., 2025)
Heavy metal removal using ensemble ML models	Adsorption	RFR, Adaboost, GB, XGBoost, LightGBM	Web-based research	The study revealed that pH and initial concentration are the main factors influencing adsorption, with an accuracy of 0.92 by XGBoost	XGBoost model metrics MSE = 0.0057, MAE = 0.0428, and the highest R2 = 0.921	Provides an effective way of using ensemble ML models for heavy metal removal	(Yaseen & Alhalimi, 2025)

(Continued)

TABLE 2.2 *(Continued)*

Applications of Machine Learning in Various Environmental Settings.

Research Purpose	Location	Model	Source of Data	Results	Metrics	Recommendations	References
Study on the anaerobic Biodegradation Rates	Bioremediation	LightGBM	Experimental	accuracy of 81%	$R^2 = 0.56$	Offers pioneer work on aerobic studies for future implementation	(Cheng et al., 2024)
Prediction of TiO2 photocatalytic degradation	Photocatalytic and Advanced Oxidation Processes	XGB, DT, LR2, SVR, AB, VR, CB, KNN and GB, RF, ANN, RR, and LR1	Literature data	The results showed that the dosage, humidity, and UV light intensity have a higher effect	R^2 values for XGB, DT, and LR2 were 0.936, 0.924, and 0.924, respectively	Provides important models to study TiO2 photocatalytic degradation	(Javed et al., 2024)
Data-driven acceleration of material design	Photocatalytic and Advanced Oxidation	LightGBM	Literature data	LightGBM can accurately predict and rank key factors controlling doped-TiO_2 photocatalytic degradation performance	$R^2 = 92.8\%$	Recommend the use of this model before actual experimental research	(Liu et al., 2022)

Assessment of forest health	Biodiversity and Ecosystem Health Assessment	DT, RF, and VSM	Experimental survey	RF provided accurate results and identified key ecological drivers	RF metrics included mean accuracy = 0.83, Kappa = 0.87, and balanced accuracy = 0.88	Study recommends restoring degraded forests and improving monitoring	(Khan et al., 2025)
Analysis of soil fertility	Soil Quality and Agricultural Productivity Monitoring	RF, MLP, and LSTM	Experimental	RF model can predict soil fertility in real-time	RF highest accuracy = 92%	Adoption of sensor-based ML and AI systems for real-time soil fertility monitoring.	(Gunasekaran et al., 2025)
Nitrate mapping in Soil	Soil Quality and Agricultural Productivity Monitoring	RFR and SVR	Experimental	RFR correctly mapped N in soils with soil organic matter as an influential predictor	RFR metrics R2 = 0.79, RMSE = 0.32, MAE = 0.18	recommends integrating ML into soil mapping for enhanced decision-making	(Auzzas, Capra, Jani, & Ganga, 2024)
Impact of climate change on forests	Climate and Weather Modelling	RF, XGBoost, and SVM	Landsat imagery database	RF model performed the best with $R^2 = 0.82$ and projected that 49–55% decline in EVI by 2040	RF metrics $R^2 = 0.82$, RMSE = 0.15	Recommends adaptive management like afforestation, policy-driven efforts, land-use planning, etc.	(Otieno, Otieno, Rotich, Löhr, & Kipkulei, 2025)
Forecasting of drought	Climate and Weather Modelling	RF, LSTM	Open-source databases	LSTM outperformed other ML modelsaccurately predicted drought conditions	LSTM metrices $R^2 = 0.766$, CC = 0.880, RMSE = 0.885	Use hybrid AI–climate modelling tools to help prepare for drought seasons	(Liu, Liu, Huang, Ren, & He, 2025)

groundwater (Lee, Ko, & Yoo, 2023; Liang, et al., 2024), with recommendations that ML models be incorporated in this field to help in predicting and mapping water contaminants. Also, in bioremediation, ML has been used to predict and optimize the production of biogas (Cheng, Zhang, Huang, & Zhang, 2024; Guo et al., 2024). The ANN and LightGBM models were used, with results revealing that the ANN accurately predicted and captured the non-linear relationships of predictors as compared to simple kinetic models.

Air quality monitoring and prediction has been another field where ML models have been utilized. For example, SVR has been employed to evaluate the air quality index and predict the particle levels in the air. An accuracy level of 94.1% was achieved with recommendations for improving its performance, and comparing its performance with other models (Castelli et al., 2020). Research conducted by Utku et al. (2025) reported an accuracy of 99.5% in the prediction of $PM_{2.5}$, which is an effective way of not only predicting but also monitoring the concentration levels of $PM_{2.5}$.

ML models have also been employed in the adsorption process to evaluate and predict the concentration levels and calculate the efficiency of removal. The use of RF in HMs evaluation in soils (Nie et al., 2024), prediction of the methylene blue dye efficiency removal (Kumari et al., 2025), and HM removal using biochar (Yaseen & Alhalimi, 2025) have all been reported as captured in the Table. An accuracy of 63%, 88.64%, and 92%, respectively, was obtained.

Furthermore, ML has been very crucial in photocatalytic and advanced oxidation processes, where it has been used to predict the photocatalytic degradation and in data-driven acceleration of material design (Javed et al., 2024; Liu et al., 2022). In biodiversity and ecosystem health assessment, DT, RF, and VSM models were employed to assess the health of forests, with RF showing a superior accuracy of 88% (Khan et al., 2025).

In soil quality and agricultural productivity monitoring, the ML has been used to analyse soil fertility and mapping of nitrate using models such as RF, MLP, LSTM, RFR, and SVR in experimentally generated datasets. High accuracy levels in soil analysis of 92% and 79% in mapping of nitrate in the soil were reported (Gunasekaran et al., 2025; Auzzas et al., 2024). Finally, in climate and weather modelling, research has been done on the impact of climate change on forests and forecasting of drought using RF, XGBoost, SVM, RF, and LSTM models. The results point to the high accuracy of 82% in the RF model and 88% in the LSTM for the impact of climate on forests and the prediction of drought, respectively (Liu et al., 2025; Otieno et al., 2025).

2.10 Conclusion and Future Recommendations

The growing adoption of ML in the field of environmental science, and more specifically in environmental monitoring and remediation, has provided a new approach that has enabled better understanding and management of the ecological systems. ML as a tool possesses great strengths like high accuracy, timely data processing, easy flexibility in scalability, and more adaptability when compared to ordinary methods. As discussed in this chapter, ML has been widely used in air, water, and soil quality monitoring, supporting the conservation of biodiversity, and providing an enhanced analysis in climate change through efficient and accurate modelling coupled to better prediction mechanisms. Despite this pronounced and remarkable progress, ML has many areas that need to be continuously improved for better ML performance. For example, there is a need to ensure that high-quality data is freely available in open environmental databases. Also, more real-time data collection using various platforms like IoT, remote sensing, and other sensing systems should be highly encouraged to help strengthen the level of prediction and offer early warnings to stakeholders. Another challenge that calls for future deliberation is addressing transparency, dealing with data bias, and addressing and explain ML techniques, which will help in improving trust, leading to acceptance and adoption among stakeholders.

References

Abebe, W., & Endalie, D. (2023). Artificial intelligence models for prediction of monthly rainfall without climatic data for meteorological stations in Ethiopia. *Journal of Big Data, 10*(1), 1–15.

Abu El-Magd, S., Soliman, G., Morsy, M., & Kharbish, S. (2023). Environmental hazard assessment and monitoring for air pollution using machine learning and remote sensing. *International Journal of Environmental Science and Technology, 20*(6), 6103–6116.

Afoma, U., Singh, S., Mishra, A., Sharma, C., Gupta, K., Mishra, M., … Sharma, V. (2025). Integrating artificial intelligence in environmental monitoring: A paradigm shift in data-driven sustainability. *EcoHealth, 23,* 38–57.

Aigbe, U., Ukhurebor, K., Onyancha, R., Emeji, I., Adeoba, M., Hassaan, M., … El Nemr, A. (2025a). Machine learning optimization of biogas production from ozonated ulva lactuca: Macromolecule degradation, energy balance, and techno-economic assessment. *Biomass and Bioenergy, 202,* 108160.

Aigbe, U., Ukhurebor, K., Onyancha, R., Osibote, A., Hassaan, M., ElKatory, M., & El Nemr, A. (2025b). Prediction of methylene blue dye sorption to sulfonated date palm kernel biochar using statistical regression and machine learning methods and DFT studies. *Journal of Molecular Liquids, 429,* 127547.

Aliferis, C., & Simon, G. (2024). Overfitting, underfitting and general model overconfidence and under-performance pitfalls and best practices in machine learning and AI. Artificial intelligence and machine learning in health care and medical sciences. In G. Simon & C. Aliferis (Eds.), *Artificial Intelligence and Machine Learning in Health Care and Medical Sciences. Health Informatics* (477–524). Cham: Springer.

Attaran, M., & Celik, B. (2023). Digital Twin: Benefits, use cases, challenges, and opportunities. *Decision Analytics Journal, 6,* 100165.

Auzzas, A., Capra, G., Jani, A., & Ganga, A. (2024). An improved digital soil mapping approach to predict total N by combining machine learning algorithms and open environmental data. *Modeling Earth Systems and Environment, 10*(5), 6519–6538.
Banerjee, A., Ó'Domhnaill, A., Creedon, L., Jones, N., & Gharbia, S. (2025). A land use regression model to explain the spatial variation of nitrate concentration–A regional scale case study in the north-west of Ireland. *Journal of Contaminant Hydrology, 270*, 104528.
Belavadi, S., Rajagopal, S., & Mohan, R. (2020). Air quality forecasting using LSTM RNN and wireless sensor networks. *Procedia Computer Science, 170*, 241–248.
Castelli, M., Clemente, F., Popovič, A., Silva, S., & Vanneschi, L. (2020). A machine learning approach to predict air quality in California. *Complexity, 2020*(1), 8049504.
Chen, G., Chen, S., Li, D., & Chen, C. (2025). A hybrid deep learning air pollution prediction approach based on neighborhood selection and spatio-temporal attention. *Scientific Reports, 15*(1), 3685.
Cheng, Y., Zhang, K., Huang, K., & Zhang, H. (2024). Meta-analysis and machine learning models for anaerobic biodegradation rates of organic contaminants in sediments and sludge. *Environmental Science & Technology, 58*(29), 12976–12988.
Cipriano, C., Noce, S., Mereu, S., & Santini, M. (2025). Algorithms going wild–A review of machine learning techniques for terrestrial ecology. *Ecological Modelling, 506*, 111164.
Dharmarathne, G., Abekoon, A., Bogahawaththa, M., Alawatugoda, J., & Meddage, D. (2025). A review of machine learning and internet-of-things on the water quality assessment: Methods, applications and future trends. *Results in Engineering, 26*, 105182.
Essam, Y., Kumar, P., Ahmed, A., Murti, M., & El-Shafie, A. (2021). Exploring the reliability of different artificial intelligence techniques in predicting earthquake for Malaysia. *Soil Dynamics and Earthquake Engineering, 147*, 106826.
Essamlali, I., Nhaila, H., & El Khaili, M. (2024). Advances in machine learning and IoT for water quality monitoring: A comprehensive review. *Heliyon, 10*(6), e27920.
Goyal, P. S. (2024). A deep learning approach for early detection of drought stress in maize using proximal scale digital images. *Neural Computing and Applications, 36*(4), 1899–1913.
Gunasekaran, K., Sreevardhan, P., & SamiKannu, R. (2025). Real-time soil fertility analysis, crop prediction, and insights using machine learning and deep learning algorithms. *Frontiers in Soil Science, 5*, 1652058.
Guo, H., Wu, F., Yang, K., Yang, Z., Chen, Z., Chen, D., & Xiao, R. (2024). Sentinel-2 multispectral satellite remote sensing retrieval of soil Cu content changes at different pH levels. *Agronomy, 14*(10), 2182.
Hao, L., Zhang, D., Zhou, H., Wang, Z., Zhang, J., Zhao, Z., & Li, M. (2025). Machine learning applications in prediction and optimization of heavy metal bioremediation: A review. *Journal of Environmental Chemical Engineering, 13*(5), 118845.
Hassan, R., & Kazemi, M. (2025). Machine learning frameworks to accurately estimate the adsorption of organic materials onto resin and biochar. *Scientific Reports, 15*(1), 15157.
Hossain, M., Shams, S., & Ullah, S. (2025). Time-series and deep learning approaches for renewable energy forecasting in Dhaka: A comparative study of ARIMA, SARIMA, and LSTM models. *Discover Sustainability, 6*(1), 1–25.
Hosseiny, B., Mahdianpari, M., Hemati, M., Radman, A., Mohammadimanesh, F., & Chanussot, J. (2023). Beyond supervised learning in remote sensing: A

systematic review of deep learning approaches. *IEEE Journal of Selected Topics in Applied Earth Observations and Remote Sensing, 17*, 1035–1052.

Janga, J., Reddy, K., & Raviteja, K. (2023). Integrating artificial intelligence, machine learning, and deep learning approaches into remediation of contaminated sites: A review. *Chemosphere, 345*, 140476.

Javed, A., Kim, T., Lee, C., Oh, J., & Han, Y. (2023). Deep learning-based detection of urban forest cover change along with overall urban changes using very-high-resolution satellite images. *Remote Sensing, 15*(17), 4285.

Javed, M., Shahab, M., Asif, U., Najeh, T., Aslam, F., Ali, M., & Khan, I. (2024). Evaluation of machine learning models for predicting TiO2 photocatalytic degradation of air contaminants. *Scientific Reports, 14*(1), 13688.

Jinbo, Z., Yufu, L., & Haitao, M. (2025). Handling missing data of using the XGBoost-based multiple imputation by chained equations regression method. *Frontiers in Artificial Intelligence, 8*, 1553220.

Jose, R., Panigrahi, S., Patil, R., Fernando, Y., & Ramakrishna, S. (2020). Artificial intelligence-driven circular economy as a key enabler for sustainable energy management. *Materials Circular Economy, 2*(1), 8.

Kazi, Z., Filip, S., & Kazi, L. (2023). Predicting PM2. 5, PM10, SO2, NO2, NO and CO air pollutant values with linear regression in R language. *Applied Sciences, 13*(6), 3617.

Khan, R., Shaheen, H., Islam Dar, M., Habib, T., Manzoor, M., Gillani, S., … Waheed, M. (2025). A data-driven approach to forest health assessment through multivariate analysis and machine learning techniques. *BMC Plant Biology, 25*(1), 915.

Kooh, M., Lim, L., Lim, L., & Malik, O. (2019). Phytoextraction potential of water fern (Azolla pinnata) in the removal of a hazardous dye, methyl violet 2B: Artificial neural network modelling. *International Journal of Phytoremediation, 20*(5), 124486.

Koukaras, P., & Tjortjis, C. (2025). Data preprocessing and feature engineering for data mining: Techniques, tools, and best practices. *AI, 6*(10), 91–99.

Kumar, P., Debele, S., Sahani, J., Rawat, N., Marti-Cardona, B., Alfieri, S., … Jaakko, J. (2021). An overview of monitoring methods for assessing the performance of nature-based solutions against natural hazards. *Earth-Science Reviews, 217*, 103603.

Kumari, S., Agarwal, S., Kumar, M., Sharma, P., Kumar, A., Hashem, A., … Garg, M. (2025). An exploration of RSM, ANN, and ANFIS models for methylene blue dye adsorption using Oryza sativa straw biomass: A comparative approach. *Scientific Reports, 15*(1), 2979.

Lakra, D., Pipil, S., Srivastava, P., Singh, S., Gupta, M., & Prasad, R. (2025). Soil moisture retrieval over agricultural region through machine learning and sentinel 1 observations. *Frontiers in Remote Sensing, 5*, 1513620.

Lee, J., Ko, K., & Yoo, K. (2023). A machine learning-based approach to predict groundwater nitrate susceptibility using field measurements and hydrogeological variables in the Nonsan Stream Watershed, South Korea. *Applied Water Science, 13*(12), 242.

Ley, A., Bormann, H., & Casper, M. (2023). Intercomparing LSTM and RNN to a conceptual hydrological model for a low-land river with a focus on the flow duration curve. *Water, 15*(3), 505.

Li, Y., Feng, Z., Chen, S., Zhao, Z., & Wang, F. (2020). Application of the artificial neural network and support vector machines in forest fire prediction in the

Guangxi autonomous region, China. *Discrete Dynamics in Nature and Society, 2020*(1), 5612650.

Liang, Y., Zhang, X., Gan, L., Chen, S. Z., Ding, J., Kang, W., & Yang, H. (2024). Mapping specific groundwater nitrate concentrations from spatial data using machine learning: A case study of Chongqing, China. *Heliyon, 10*(6), e27867.

Liu, J., Liu, T., Huang, L., Ren, Y., & He, P. (2025). Next-generation drought forecasting: Hybrid AI models for climate resilience. *Remote Sensing, 17*(20), 340.

Liu, Q., Pan, K., Lu, Y., Wei, W., Wang, S., Du, W., … Zhou, Y. (2022). Data-driven for accelerated design strategy of photocatalytic degradation activity prediction of doped TiO_2 photocatalyst. *Journal of Water Process Engineering, 49*, 103126.

Ma, W., Cui, J., Abdoulaye, B., Wang, Y., Du, H., Bourtsalas, A., & Chen, G. (2022). Air pollutant emission inventory of waste-to-energy plants in China and prediction by the artificial neural network approach. *Environmental Science & Technology, 57*(2), 874–883.

Maharana, K., Mondal, S., & Nemade, B. (2022). A review: Data pre-processing and data augmentation techniques. *Global Transitions Proceedings, 3*(1), 91–99.

Majid, A., Ikhsan, N., & Hassan, Z. (2025). Utility of satellite imagery in estimating coastal marine water attributes. *Continental Shelf Research, 292*, 105509. https://doi.org/10.1016/j.csr.2025.105509

Manikandan, G., & Abirami, S. (2021). An efficient feature selection framework based on information theory for high dimensional data. *Applied Soft Computing, 111*, 107729.

Messaoud, S., Bradai, A., Bukhari, S., Quang, P., Ahmed, O., & Atri, M. (2020). A survey on machine learning in internet of things: Algorithms, strategies, and applications. *Internet of Things, 12*, 100314.

Meza, J., Yepes, D., Rodrigo-Ilarri, J., & Cassiraga, E. (2019). Predictive analysis of urban waste generation for the city of Bogotá, Colombia, through the implementation of decision trees-based machine learning, support vector machines and artificial neural networks. *Heliyon, 5*(11), e02810.

Mishra, A. (2025). Internet of things-based sensors for environmental monitoring. In J. McLaughlin, A. Mathur & S. M. Tauseef (Eds.), *Emerging sensors for environmental monitoring* (167–186). Elsevier.

Mohammadi, F., Samaei, M., Azhdarpoor, A., Teiri, H., Badeenezhad, A., & Rostami, S. (2019). Modelling and optimizing pyrene removal from the soil by phytoremediation using response surface methodology, artificial neural networks, and genetic algorithm. *Chemosphere, 237*, 124486.

Mohd Zebaral Hoque, J., Ab. Aziz, N., Alelyani, S., Mohana, M., & Hosain, M. (2022). Improving water quality index prediction using regression learning models. *International Journal of Environmental Research and Public Health, 19*(20), 13702.

Montesinos López, O., Montesinos López, A., & Crossa, J. (2022). Overfitting, model tuning, and evaluation of prediction performance. In O. A. M. López, A. M. López & J. Crossa (Eds.), *Multivariate statistical machine learning methods for genomic prediction* (109–139). Cham: Springer International Publishing.

Ndiaye, A., Shen, Y., Kyriakou, K., Karssenberg, D., Schmitz, O., Flückiger, B., … Hoek, G. (2024). Hourly land-use regression modeling for NO2 and PM2. 5 in the Netherlands. *Environmental Research, 256*, 119233.

Nguyen, T., Grote, U., Neubacher, F., Do, M., & Paudel, G. (2023). Security risks from climate change and environmental degradation: Implications for sustainable land use transformation in the Global South. *Current Opinion in Environmental Sustainability, 63*, 101322.

Nie, S., Chen, H., Sun, X., & An, Y. (2024). Spatial distribution prediction of soil heavy metals based on a random forest model. *Sustainability, 16*(11), 4358.

Niroomand, M., Pahlavani, P., Bigdeli, B., & Ghorbanzadeh, O. (2025). Improving the temporal Resolution of land surface temperature using machine and deep learning models. *Geomatics, 5*(4), 50.

Noori, A., Ziboon, A., & AL-Hameedawi, A. (2025). Deep-learning integration of CNN–Transformer and U-net for bi-temporal SAR flash-flood detection. *Applied Sciences, 15*(14), 7770.

Olawade, D., Wada, O., Ige, A., Egbewole, B., Olojo, A., & Oladapo, B. (2024). Artificial intelligence in environmental monitoring: Advancements, challenges, and future directions. *Hygiene and Environmental Health Advances, 12*, 100114.

Otieno, T., Otieno, L., Rotich, B., Löhr, K., & Kipkulei, H. (2025). Modeling climate change impacts and predicting future vulnerability in the Mount Kenya forest ecosystem using remote sensing and machine learning. *Environmental Monitoring and Assessment, 197*(6), 631.

Özüpak, Y., Alpsalaz, F., & Aslan, E. (2025). Air quality forecasting using machine learning: Comparative analysis and ensemble strategies for enhanced prediction. *Water, Air, & Soil Pollution, 236*(7), 464.

Panigrahi, N., Patro, S., Kumar, R., Omar, M., Ngan, T., Giang, N., … Thang, N. (2023). Groundwater quality analysis and drinkability prediction using artificial intelligence. *Earth Science Informatics, 16*(2), 1701–1725.

Parlak, B., & Yavaşoğlu, H. (2023). Comparison of regression algorithms to predict average air temperature. *International Journal of Engineering Research and Development, 15*(1), 312–322.

Parveen, N., Zaidi, S., & Danish, M. (2019). Support vector regression (SVR)-based adsorption model for ni (II) ions removal. *Groundwater for Sustainable Development, 9*, 100232.

Pianosi, F., Beven, K., Freer, J., Hall, J., Rougier, J., Stephenson, D., & Wagener, T. (2016). Sensitivity analysis of environmental models: A systematic review with practical workflow. *Environmental Modelling & Software, 79*, 214–232.

Piao, Y., Lee, D., Park, S., Kim, H., & Jin, Y. (2022). Forest fire susceptibility assessment using google earth engine in Gangwon-do, Republic of Korea. *Geomatics, Natural Hazards and Risk, 13*(1), 432–450.

Pino Santana, A., Garcia-Gen, S., Dewasme, L., & Vande Wouwer, A. (2025). Model predictive control of anaerobic digestion processes using a long short-term memory network predictor. *Water Science & Technology, 92*(7), 1063–1076.

Rosales, C., R, Bratburd, J., Diez, S., Duncan, S., Malings, C., & Pant, P. (2025). Open air quality data platforms for environmental health research and action. *Current Environmental Health Reports, 12*(1), 27.

Sang, G., Xu, L., & de Vrieze, P. (2021). A predictive maintenance model for flexible manufacturing in the context of industry. *Frontiers in Big Data, 4*, 663466.

Sierra-Porta, D. (2024). Assessing the impact of missing data on water quality index estimation: A machine learning approach. *Discover Water, 4*(1), 11.

Sinha, P., Sahu, D., Prakash, S., Yang, T., Rathore, R., & Pandey, V. (2025). A high performance hybrid LSTM CNN secure architecture for IoT environments using deep learning. *Scientific Reports, 15*(1), 9684.

Song, J., Gao, J., Zhang, Y. L., Man, W., Liu, M., Wang, J., … Li, C. (2022). Estimation of soil organic carbon content in coastal wetlands with measured VIS-NIR spectroscopy using optimized support vector machines and random forests. *Remote Sensing, 14*(17), 4372.

Soori, M., Arezoo, B., & Dastres, R. (2023). Artificial intelligence, machine learning and deep learning in advanced robotics, a review. *Cognitive Robotics, 3,* 54–70.

Stephen, O. (2024). Emerging technology integration-artificial intelligence (AI) and machine learning (ML) for predictive analysis for safety and toxicity assessment in environmental toxicology. *International Journal of Scientific Research and Management, 12*(5), 1182–1195.

Umutoni, L., & Samadi, V. (2024). Application of machine learning approaches in supporting irrigation decision making: A review. *Agricultural Water Management, 294,* 108710.

Utku, A., Can, U., Alpsülün, M., Balıkçı, H., Amoozegar, A., Pilatin, A., & Barut, A. (2025). Advancing air quality monitoring: Deep learning-based CNN-RNN hybrid model for PM2. 5 forecasting. *Atmosphere, 16*(9), 1003.

Velenturf, A., & Purnell, P. (2021). Principles for a sustainable circular economy. *Sustainable Production and Consumption, 27,* 1437–1457.

Wali, S., Khan, M., Zhang, M., & Shakoor, A. (2025). Genetic algorithm-based hybrid deep learning framework for stability prediction of ABO3 perovskites in solar cell applications. *Energies, 18*(19), 5052.

Wang, W., Wang, G., Li, J., Chen, J., Gao, Z., Fang, L., … Wang, Q. (2025). Remote sensing identification and model-based prediction of harmful algal blooms in inland waters: Current insights and future perspectives. *Water Research X, 28,* 100369.

Wang, Z., Wu, X., & Wu, Y. (2023). A spatiotemporal XGBoost model for PM2. 5 concentration prediction and its application in Shanghai. *Heliyon, 9*(12), e22569.

Yaseen, Z., & Alhalimi, F. (2025). Heavy metal adsorption efficiency prediction using biochar properties: A comparative analysis for ensemble machine learning models. *Scientific Reports, 15*(1), 13434.

Ye, Z., Yang, J., Zhong, N., Tu, X., Jia, J., & Wang, J. (2020). Tackling environmental challenges in pollution controls using artificial intelligence: A review. *Science of the Total Environment, 699,* 134279.

Zagajewski, B., Kluczek, M., Raczko, E., Njegovec, A., Dabija, A., & Kycko, M. (2021). Comparison of random forest, support vector machines, and neural networks for post-disaster forest species mapping of the krkonoše/karkonosze transboundary biosphere reserve. *Remote Sensing, 13*(13), 2581.

Zakaria, M., Malek, M., Zolkepli, M., & Ahmed, A. (2021). Application of artificial intelligence algorithms for hourly river level forecast: A case study of Muda River, Malaysia. *Alexandria Engineering Journal, 60*(4), 4015–4028.

Zhao, B., Zhu, W., Hao, S., Hua, M., Liao, Q., Jing, Y., … Gu, X. (2023). Prediction heavy metals accumulation risk in rice using machine learning and mapping pollution risk. *Journal of Hazardous Materials, 448,* 130879.

3

Machine Learning-Driven Environmental Monitoring Systems in Air, Water, and Soil

Abstract

The increasing intricacy of ecological contamination (CTN) in air, water, and soil bionetworks requires unconventional, information-driven monitoring (MG) and management solutions. Outmoded approaches of ecological assessment often suffer from limitations, for instance, low spatial and time-based resolution, delayed response times, and high working expenses. Current developments in machine learning (ML) have transformed ecological MG by allowing computerized information processing, analytical modelling, and intelligent decision-making (DM). This chapter explores the incorporation of ML algorithms (ALGMs) with sensing technologies (TECHs) for all-inclusive ecological observation. In the MG of air quality, ML models (Ms) are exploited for contaminant source identification, forecast of particulate matter concentrations, and the assessment of climate impact. For water systems, ML allows for the detection of pollutants, optimization of treatment processes, and instantaneous water quality prediction using Internet of Things (IoT)-based sensors. In soil MG, ML supports the assessment of pollution (PLN) levels, nutrient mapping, and sustainable agricultural administration. The book chapter also deliberates on associated challenges like data heterogeneity, model interpretability, and the requirement for standardized information sets. Overall, ML-driven systems demonstrate substantial potential to improve ecological protection, encourage sustainability, and support data-informed policy development.

3.1 Introduction

Changing faster than ever is the bionetwork. Considering our environmental state is central to protecting it more efficiently. Ecological challenges like deforestation, contamination (CTN) of the ocean, biodiversity loss, and change in climate characterize substantial threats to the world's bionetworks and the health of humans. No longer distant uncertainties but day-to-day

DOI: 10.1201/9781003618584-3

certainties in many parts of the biosphere are the rising temperature, water scarcity, land degradation, and poor quality of air. Recognizing these variations in time to react has always been a task. Conventional monitoring (MG) approaches are often too sluggish, inadequate, or exclusive to capture the full representation. The well-being of the natural bionetworks, as well as water, soil, air, and the bionetworks, is tracked using environmental MG, by assessing the levels of CTN, chemical composition, and temperature. This information assists in identifying precincts of concern that require the needed attention. Artifical intelligence (AI) enhances this process by analysing a huge amount of information from sources like "sensors, drones and satellite images". With this information, authorities can move more from responsive observation to practical intervention and make swift, more well-versed decisions to guard the earth and its inhabitants (Alotaibi & Nassif, 2024; Sand Technologies, 2023).

A key process to assessing and moderating the impact of human actions on the bionetwork is referred to as environmental MG. It comprises of the methodical observation, evaluation, and assessment of different ecological components to sense variations that may pose hazards to the stability of the bionetwork and communal health. The environmental MGs main objective is to create baseline settings, monitor changes over time and recognize possible ecological risks to apprise policy choices and justification of approaches. Conventionally, ecological monitoring (EMG) depends on procedures like statistical research, physical SMLG, and laboratory testing. While these approaches have been influential in ecological evaluation, they are often controlled by substantial restrictions, such as high working budgets, time-consuming information gathering processes, tasks in accomplishing high precision all-inclusive information collection, and the lack of openness around information, as depicted by Figure 3.1. Constraints generally result in MG plans with a trivial scope, a smaller sample size, and an inability to offer a comprehensive illustration of the ecological settings. Therefore, serious ecological variations may go unnoticed or acknowledged too late for efficient intervention (Afoma et al., 2025; Ogidi, Onwuagba, & Richard-Nwachukwu, 2024; Olawade et al., 2024; Shalu, 2023).

Another key drawback of traditional MG approaches is the substantial amount of time needed for information gathering, processing, and examination. Holdups in getting results can hamper timely policymaking, especially in situations where instantaneous action is needed to avoid ecological degradation or alleviate community health risks. Furthermore, the possibility of human-error and discrepancies in the quality of information is increased with the dependence on laboratory-based studies and physical SMLG (Afoma et al., 2025; Li et al., 2020; Olawade et al., 2024). Organizations liable for protecting the bionetwork must devote time and money to collecting ecological information from several sources before making it public. Accurate and reliable verification of information is time-restricted, and the absence of communication and partnership among departments renders the gathered

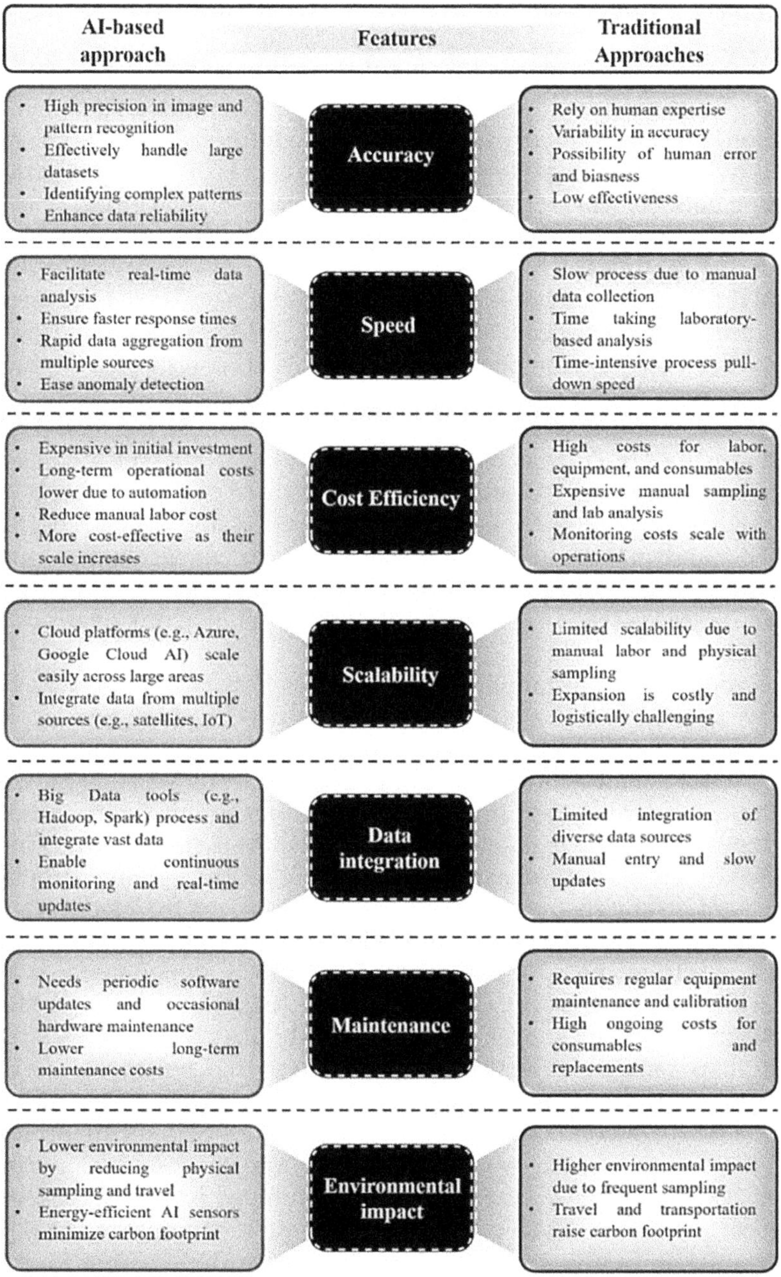

FIGURE 3.1
Comparative outline of AI-based and outmoded methods in EMG. The figure links AI-based and outmoded EMG methods transversely in seven important metrics, stressing AI's strong point in "precision, speed, scalability, and cost-efficiency", in addition to its potential to decrease ecological effect and support significant mechanization. (From Afoma et al. (2025), Springer Nature With Permission.)

environmental protection information useless from a corporate viewpoint (Shalu, 2023).

However, the effective application of accurate EMG hinges heavily on the accessibility of cutting-edge TECHs and effectively trained staff. But, fiscal limitations and a scarcity of trained professionals frequently pose substantial hurdles to implementing classy MG systems. This task is chiefly noticeable in emerging nations, where inadequate infrastructure and technical know-how further deter the active ecological observation programs institution. Thus, routine and significant EMG remains problematic to attain in numerous parts of the biosphere, theoretically compromising hard work to address ecological problems appropriately and efficiently. Addressing these drawbacks requires the incorporation of contemporary TECHs and pioneering methodologies to improve the efficiency, precision, and scalability of EMG systems (Figure 3.1). Emerging developments like automation, AI, big data (BD), and remote sensing TECHs offer capable solutions to overcome the inefficiency of outmoded approaches. Notwithstanding that these TECHs enable instantaneous MG, which also enhances information processing abilities, permitting more DM and practical environmental management. Ecological information sharing and comparison, encouraging openness and transparency, are allowed by these TECHs (Afoma et al., 2025; Li et al., 2020; Olawade et al., 2024; Shalu, 2023).

In current years, substantial progressions in EMG and information scrutiny have been achieved with the convergence of AI and ML with ecological science. These TECHs provide powerful tools to address intricate ecological tasks by ensuring more precise forecasts, instantaneous MG, and the capability to assess enormous information sets that conventional approaches cannot achieve effectively (Alotaibi & Nassif, 2024). AI is starting to restructure how we see and guard the earth. Its capability to analyse huge amounts of information instantaneously is supporting researchers to detect CTN, track deforestation, and forecast faster and more precisely than ever before climate changes. AI-driven EMG offers an accessible, practical path towards a more justifiable future (Aigbe et al., 2021; Onyancha, Aigbe, Ukhurebor, & Muchiri, 2021; Sand Technologies, 2023; Ukhurebor et al., 2021).

Central to safeguarding the bionetwork and the health of humans is environmental MG. Artificial Intelligence (AI) emergence, precisely Deep-Learning (DL) Convolutional Neural Networks (CNNs), has enhanced object recognition and identification from image information sets, narrowing the gap between machine capabilities and humans. AI has developed as a vital incorporation in EMG purposes, in the quest to improve the objectivity of results and enhance accessibility to areas suffering from inadequate resources. It is a subfield of computer science (CS), which prominences focuses on producing ALGMs and computer-programs that can achieve activities such as reasoning, learning, sensing, and DM that would normally need human intelligence. By leveraging AI TECHs, the process of MG can be accelerated, improving productivity and precision in evaluating ecological settings. Generally, incorporating information-driven methods and AI TECHs into land use planning and EMG can greatly improve DM and contribute to sustainable practices of land management (Olawade et al., 2024; Shalu, 2023).

For illustration, AI (ML) has been used to model the effects of the change in climate, like the global rise in temperature, increased extreme weather events frequency, and the rise of sea level, which threaten seaside residents and bionetworks. A key driver of biodiversity loss and carbon emission is deforestation, and has been broadly observed by utilizing AI models (Ms) that examine satellite imagery and real-time detection of illegal logging activities. The CTN of the ocean from plastic waste poses severe hazards to the aquatic bionetworks, and AI-driven TECHs are applied to detect and track CTN in coastal waters and the open sea, recognizing CTN patterns (PATs) and sources more efficiently. These ecological challenges high spot the vital requirement for pioneering solutions, and AI/ML approaches provide effective, automated, and scalable solutions (Alotaibi & Nassif, 2024).

Conventionally, numerical Ms have been important tools in soil and water management. But their dependence on a restricted set of variables and detailed assumptions often results in prediction accuracy being greatly dependent on the given input information. Furthermore, they may flop to justify uncertainties in climate change detection. Accordingly, cutting-edge tools that can accompany or even substitute for outmoded numerical Ms are desirable. Incorporation of ML and remote sensing (RS) information offers an auspicious solution to the restrictions of outmoded approaches in soil and water management (Kim et al., 2024).

This book's interest in ML-driven environmental monitoring systems applications (APLs) in air, water, and soil has significantly improved in modern times, and there is a requirement to have a diverse look into these thrust areas. Diverse scientific literatures are included within the field of science and are recognized across numerous catalogues such as PubMed, Microsoft Academic Web of Science, Dimensions, Scopus, and Google Scholar. Scopus was selected by the authors of this review article to be applied, due to its all-inclusive peer-reviewed research journals and citations in this field from various international journals (Halevi, Moed, & Bar-Ilan, 2017; Mezquita, Martín-Delgado, Wennberg-Capellades, & Borrego, 2025; Padhiary, Saha, Kumar, Sethi, & Kumar, 2024). Scopus information sources are 100% all-encompassing of PubMed and are maintained by Elsevier. It consists of twice the amount of journal catalogues in the WOS (Sweileh, 2021). To track scholarly literature and to establish the influence of publication in relation to citations, bibliographic information sources are utilized by researchers (Mezquita et al., 2025). A bibliometric study was implemented in VOSviewer using the methodology of Padhiary et al., 2024. The VOSviewer visualization map shows a network of how research topics related to machine learning-driven (MLD) environmental MG systems are interconnected. Clearly, we can see four clusters, namely blue, green, red, and yellow, as displayed

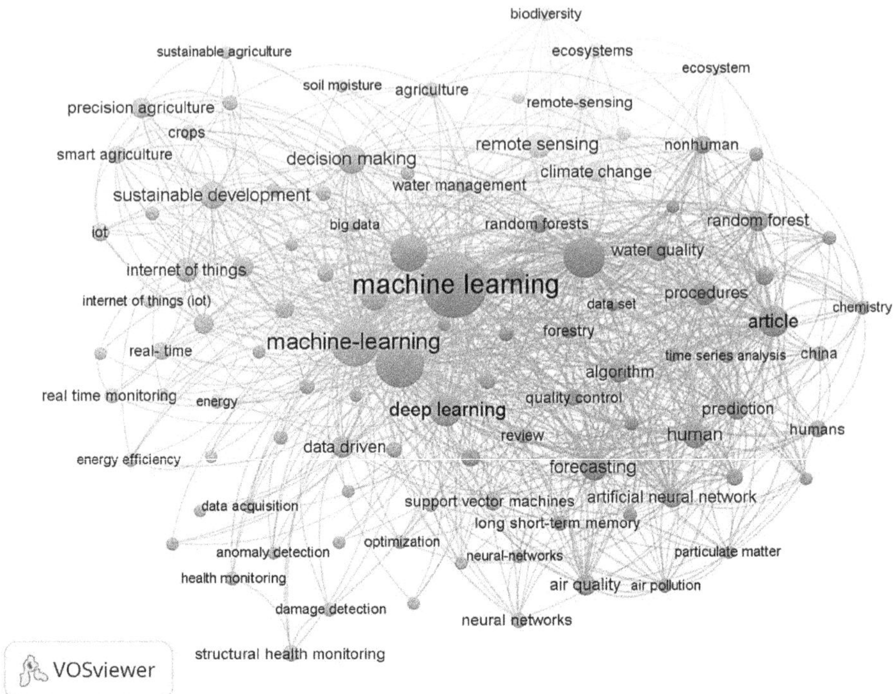

FIGURE 3.2
The keyword network diagram is based on 976 journal articles retrieved from the Scopus catalogue with the keyword "ML and Environmental MG Systems".

in Figure 3.2. The blue cluster is centred on ML and DL. This part covers all key methods and ALGMs (support vector machines, NNs, data-driven approaches, anomaly detection, and structural health MG) that are related to environmental MG. The green cluster shows the connection of ML to applied environmental MG areas, particularly in agricultural and resource management. This group is characterized by terms such as IoT, real-time MG, energy efficiency, sustainability, precision agriculture, and smart agriculture, which all point to the ML APLs. The red cluster covers the methodological aspects and specific environmental APLs. They are tied with literary words and phrases like forecasting, quality control, air PLN, air quality, and particle matter, which emphasize a given application/specific topic. The yellow links the broader environmental science topics like remote sensing, ecosystems, climate change, biodiversity, and water management. This cluster tries to show an intersection of ML with ecosystem MG and remote sensing. Table 3.1 gives the cluster colour, themes, and keywords as extracted from the VOSviewer map. This chapter seeks to broadly examine and assess the present state of AI TECHs applied in EMG, with a key focus on their effectiveness. There was

TABLE 3.1

Cluster Colour, Themes, and Keywords as Extracted from the VOSviewer Map

Cluster Colour	Themes	Keywords
Blue	Methods and ALGMs	ML, DL, optimization, anomaly detection
Green	IoT and Applied MG	IoT, real-time MG, precision agriculture, sustainable development
Red	Literature and Specific APLs.	Forecasting, quality control, air quality, prediction, article
Yellow	Environmental Science and Remote Sensing	Remote sensing, climate change, water quality, ecosystems, biodiversity

an upward trend in the amount of publications that were indexed in Scopus from 2015–2025 (November), based on the keywords used for search (MLD and Environmental MG Systems). There were a noticeable twofold increase and reduction in the number of published articles from 2015–2017, and 2017–November 2025 (Figure 3.3).

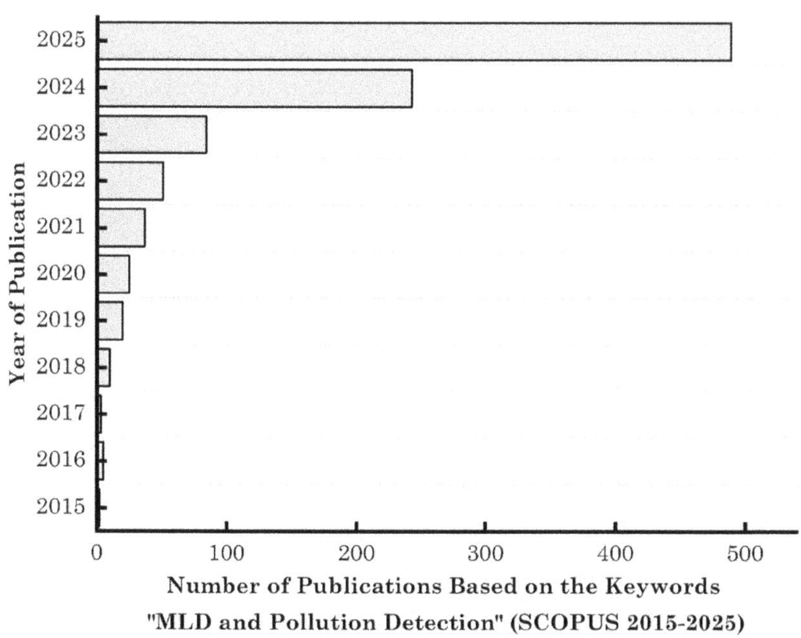

FIGURE 3.3
Scientific publications trend in the Scopus information source on MLD for environmental MG systems from 2015 to November 2025.

3.2 AI for Environmental MG

AI has developed as a vital incorporation in EMG purposes, in the quest to improve the objectivity of results and enhance accessibility to areas suffering from inadequate resources. It is a sub-field of CS, which prominences focuses on producing ALGMs and computer programs that can achieve activities such as learning, reasoning, sensing, and DM that would normally need human intelligence. Huge information sets can be analysed by applying AI, which has been established to be suitable for pattern identification and making specific forecasts. In EMG, it has been used in different areas such as natural disaster forecasting, air, and water quality MG and contaminants recognition. Table 3.2 gives a comparative study of AI approaches against conventional methods in terms of speed, scalability, information incorporation, maintenance, precision, and ecological effect. The substantial benefits of AI in improving the competence and usefulness of environmental MG are underscored by AI while considering the possible opening costs and the position of considering long-term advantages (Olawade et al., 2024; Srivastava & Sharma, 2024).

Furthermore, the use of these unconventional TECHs and the existence of suitably trained technical staff are required for the exact EMG is regularly hampered by the cost limitations and shortage of competent persons. Therefore, the fulfilment of regular MG becomes a laborious task, specifically in areas of the world facing resource constraints, predominantly in developing countries. Hence, in current years, AI has appeared as a central incorporation in EMG endeavours, in the quest to improve the independence of results and enhance accessibility to areas suffering from restricted resources (Shalu, 2023).

3.3 Important Benefits of Applying AI (ML) in EMG Systems

Ecological AI offers various benefits that assist in tracking variations and enhance MG efforts more effectively than conventional approaches. The following advancements allow authorities to act more readily, improve resource administration, and provide more justifiable solutions (Sand Technologies, 2023).

3.3.1 Instantaneous Information Gathering and Analysis

The ability of AI in environmental MG to process information in real-time is a key benefit. In a period when environmental variations like natural adversities can happen swiftly, it is essential to be able to track and examine these events in actual time. AI power-driven systems can observe everything

TABLE 3.2

AI Approaches Set against Outmoded Methods in EMG

Measures	AI Approaches (Detailed Model/Tool)	Outmoded Approaches
Precision	**DL** Ms **(CNNs)**: High accuracy in the recognition of images and PATs **Random Forests**: Efficient for handling huge information sets and recognizing multifaceted PATs **"Support Vector Machines (SVM)"**: Outstanding for cataloguing responsibilities	Variable precision is reliant on human know-how Vulnerable to human mistakes and prejudices Regularly restricted by the resolution and frequency of physical sampling (SMLG)
Speed	**"Instantaneous Information Processing (TensorFlow and Keras)"**: Instantaneous examination and anomaly recognition **Automatic** MG **Systems (IBM Watson)**: Quicker information combination and synthesis from numerous sources	Time-consuming information gathering and examination Deferred results owing to prolonged laboratory-processes Sluggish response-time in emergency circumstances
Cost	Preliminary setup can be exclusive (software, equipment, and training) Longstanding working costs are lower owing to computerization and the condensed requirement for human labour Scalable with declining marginal budgets	Highly elevated continuing costs for labour, paraphernalia, and consumables Exclusive physical SMLG and laboratory studies Expenses rise correspondingly with the measure of MG efforts
Scalability	**Cloud-based platforms (Microsoft Azure and Google Cloud AI)**: Simply scalable to cover huge geographic zones. Accomplished by incorporating information from several sources, like satellites and IoT devices	Inadequate scalability owing to dependence on human labour and physical SMLG Exclusive and logistically thought-provoking to enlarge coverage
Information Incorporation	BD **Analytics Tools like Hadoop and Apache-Spark**: Handle and incorporate large volumes of diverse data. Accomplished continuous MG and instantaneous updates	Restricted capacity to incorporate various information sources Physical information entry and slower information updates
Maintenance	Needs intermittent software-updates and infrequent hardware maintenance Lesser maintenance costs over time	Systematic equipment maintenance and calibration Elevated unending costs for consumables and replacements
Ecological Effect	Lesser ecological impact owing to condensed requirement for manual SMLG and travel **Energy-effective solutions, such as AI-powered sensors**, lessen the carbon-footprint	Higher ecological impact from recurrent manual SMLG Travel and transportation rise carbon-footprint

(Continued)

TABLE 3.2 *(Continued)*

AI Approaches Set against Outmoded Methods in EMG

Measures	AI Approaches (Detailed Model/Tool)	Outmoded Approaches
Precision	**DL** Ms **(CNNs)**: High accuracy in the recognition of images and PATs **Random Forests**: Efficient for handling huge information sets and recognizing multifaceted PATs **Support Vector Machines (SVM)**: Outstanding for cataloguing tasks	Variable precision is reliant on human know-how Vulnerable to human mistakes and biases Regularly restricted by the resolution and frequency of physical SMLG
Speed	**Instantaneous Information Processing (TensorFlow and Keras)**: Instantaneous examination and anomaly recognition **Automatic** MG **Systems (IBM Watson)**: Quicker information combination and synthesis from numerous sources	Time-intensive information gathering and examination Deferred results owing to prolonged laboratory processes Sluggish response time in emergency circumstances
Cost	Preliminary setup can be exclusive (software, equipment, and training) Longstanding working costs are lower owing to computerization and the condensed requirement for human labour Scalable with declining marginal budgets	Highly elevated continuing costs for labour, equipment, and consumables Exclusive physical SMLG and laboratory studies Costs rise correspondingly with the measure of MG efforts
Scalability	**Cloud-based Platforms (Microsoft Azure and Google Cloud AI)**: Simply scalable to cover huge geographic zones Capable of incorporating information from several sources, like satellites and IoT devices	Inadequate scalability owing to dependence on human labour and physical SMLG Exclusive and logistically thought-provoking to enlarge coverage
Information Incorporation	BD **Analytics Tools like Hadoop and Apache Spark**: Handle and incorporate large volumes of diverse data Accomplished continuous MG and instantaneous updates	Restricted capacity to incorporate various information sources Physical information entry and slower information updates
Maintenance	Needs intermittent software updates and infrequent hardware maintenance Lesser maintenance costs over time	Systematic equipment maintenance and calibration Elevated unending costs for consumables and replacements
Ecological Effect	Lesser ecological impact owing to condensed requirement for manual SMLG and travel **Energy-effective solutions, such as AI-powered sensors**, lessen the carbon-footprint	Higher ecological impact from recurrent manual SMLG Travel and transportation rise carbon-footprint

from the quality of air to seismic action, permitting researchers to observe changes instantly and act before conditions deteriorate. The speed is central in situations such as floods or serious storms, and wildfires, where timing decreases damage and life loss (Olawade et al., 2024; Sand Technologies, 2023). A better example of this information allowed MG is the EcoRisk Visualizer tool. This tool assists stakeholders in reducing CTN hazards by incorporating several information sources and modelling intricate setups. It allows a decrease in sewage pumping station CTN by up to 50% and assists in cutting CTN-associated clean-up expenses and regulatory fines by over 20% via analytical, information-driven understandings (Sand Technologies, 2023).

3.3.2 Precise Predicting and Risk Justification

With the continuous global change, insights and anticipating future leanings are critical for planning efficient preventative procedures. A substantial role is played by AI in ecological prediction by analysing past information to forecast imminent events. For example, AI can provide extremely precise forecasts in the insurance industry, where firms are required to develop strategies for natural catastrophes or climate-associated risks. These understandings allow improved DM, enabling more efficient implementation of risk moderation approaches earlier. Also, AI and IoT power-driven forecasting tools like the Hydraulic Network Risk Tool can assist in decreasing the fiscal and human cost of events in the environment. This tool is used in the UK by the largest private water services to predict possible water outages, allowing preventative action that saves the UK government 7 million pounds (Kumar, 2024; Olawade et al., 2024; Sand Technologies, 2023).

3.3.3 Amplified Effectiveness in MG Schemes

A key source of ecological impairment is the ageing infrastructure. As these systems decline, there is a drop in their performance, and there is an increased risk of causing substantial ecological harm. The efficiency of equipment and MG systems is improved by AI, by guaranteeing they stay in top shape. By applying predictive maintenance devices, the condition of sensors, drones, and other MG tools can be tracked using AI, signalling when maintenance or replacements are required. This tracking assists in safeguarding that these systems remain functioning and reduces idle time, permitting nonstop and precise MG (Chisom et al., 2024; Jain, 2024; Sand Technologies, 2023).

3.3.4 Scalable Solution to Ecological Tasks

Principally valuable for tracking extensive ecological tasks is AI. AI permits scientists and conservationists to act before problems escalate, with early warnings about ecological hazards. AI can offer solutions that are flexible to various areas and tasks, whether it is responding to water CTN, or a change in climate and deforestation (Sand Technologies, 2023).

3.4 TECHs Behind Environmental MG Using AI

No longer out of reach are the insights about the environment without being physically existing in every place. Ecological AI brings together controlling TECHs that assemble, scrutinize, and interpret information from far and wide. Discussed in the subsection are the various AI tools applied in environmental MG (Reynolds et al., 2025; Sand Technologies, 2023).

3.4.1 Machine Learning (ML)

We live in the information age, where everything around us is linked to an information source, and everything in human lives is numerically documented. The information can be structured, unstructured, and semi-structured. Increasing day by day are the types of real-world information and ML approaches. Extracting understanding from this information can be applied to build several intelligent APLs in the applicable fields. Artificial intelligence (AI), mainly ML, has grown swiftly in current years in the information study and computing context, which characteristically permits the APLs to function intelligently. ML generally offers systems with the capacity to automatically learn and improve from experience without being precisely programmed and is generally referred to as the most widespread TECHs in the "Fourth Industrial Revolution (Industry 4.0 or 4IR)". 4IR is generally the unending automation of traditional manufacturing and industrial practices, comprising of exploratory information processing, applying novel smart TECHs like ML automation. Hence, to logically examine this information and to create the equivalent real-world uses, ML ALGMs are important (Sarker, 2021a; Sarker, 2021b; Sarker, 2022).

Examining historical information to predict ecological threats like life-threatening weather or species extermination is carried out using ML. Analytical modelling examines various situations, assisting scientists in planning for risks such as droughts and growing sea levels (Olawade et al., 2024; Sand Technologies, 2023). ML is a subfield of AI that concentrates on ALGMs and statistical Ms' creation, which permit computer systems to learn from information and make forecasts or decisions based on the information. ML's purpose is to produce systems that can improve their work performance without being obviously trained to do so. ML algorithm types comprise of "unsupervised, supervised, semi-supervised, and reinforcement learning", as shown in Figure 3.4 (Sand Technologies, 2023; Sarker, 2021a; Taye, 2023). In

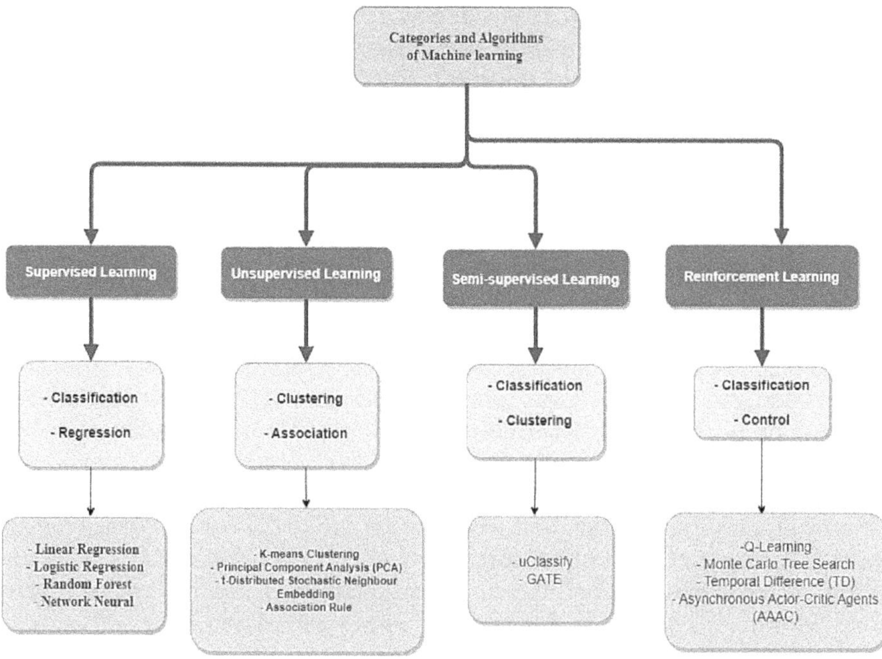

FIGURE 3.4
Several categories of ML methods. (From Taye (2023), Attribution 4.0 International, licensed under the terms and conditions of the Creative Commons Attribution (CC BY 4.0) license (http://creativecommons.org/licenses/by/4.0/)).

supervised learning, the characteristic task of ML is to study a function that plots an input to an output based on the sample pairs of input and output. It utilizes labelled training information and a gathering of training instances to deduce a function. Supervised learning is performed when certain goals are recognized to be accomplished from a certain input set, like task task-driven method. The most common task of supervised learning is classification, which separates the information and regression that fits the information (Jiang, Gradus, & Rosellini, 2020; Sarker, 2021b). This method is generally beneficial for tasks such as air quality level prediction or vegetation type categorization in a satellite image. Common ALGMs in supervised learning consist of NNs, decision trees (DTs), and SV Machines (SVMs) (Alotaibi & Nassif, 2024).

Unsupervised learning examines unlabelled information sets without the requirement for human meddling, such as an information-driven procedure. This is generally applied in the generative structures extraction, classifying expressive tendencies and structures, groupings in results and exploratory purposes. The most regular unsupervised learning tasks are density estimation, feature learning, clustering, detection of anomalies, dimensionality decrease, finding association rules, and so on (Sarker, 2021a). The goal of unsupervised learning is to infer the natural structure existing within a set of information points. This can be useful for clustering similar CTN sources or detecting anomalies in ecological information. Typical examples of "unsupervised learning approaches" are the k-means clustering and principal component analysis (PCA) algorithm (Alotaibi & Nassif, 2024).

In this category of learning, the given information is a blend of unclassified and classified information. In semi-supervised learning, it is described as a hybridization of the unsupervised and supervised approaches, as it operates on both labelled and unlabelled information, which is employed to create a suitable model for the information organization (Bhowmick, Narvekar, & Khatkhatay, 2019; Mohammed, Khan, & Bashier, 2016; Sarker, 2021b; Shakya, Alavi, Porteous, Laddi, & Jaiswal, 2024). Hence, it falls between learning with supervision and without supervision. In the context of the real world, labelled information is uncommon in numerous settings, and unlabelled information is copious, where semi-supervised learning is valuable. The semi-supervised definitive goal is to provide an improved outcome for the forecast than that formed employing the labelled information from the model. The way we learn is similar to the semi learning process. Machine translation, detection of fraud, information labelling, and classification of text are some useful areas where semi-supervised learning is applied (Sarker, 2021b).

In reinforcement learning, an ML algorithm type allows software agents and machines to routinely assess the optimal behaviour in a certain context or environment to enhance their effectiveness, such as an environment-driven method. This learning type is hinge on penalties or rewards, and its definitive goal is to utilize understanding gained from ecological campaigners to act to improve the reward or lessen the risk (Kamble et al., 2025; Sarker, 2021a). It is a controlling device for training AI Ms that can assist in improving robotics or optimizing the working efficiency of sophisticated systems like manufacturing, supply chain logistics, self-governing driving tasks, and robotics. Hence, to build efficient Ms in different application fields, different categories of ML approaches can play a substantial part according to their learning capacities, depending on the nature of information and target result (Sarker, 2021b; Thenmozhi & Krisknakumari, 2024; Toorajipour, Sohrabpour, Nazarpour, Oghazi, & Fischl, 2021). This method can be used to optimize ecological management approaches, like creating policies for decreasing emissions or handling natural resources sustainably (Alotaibi & Nassif, 2024).

An algorithm is trained utilizing considered information in supervised learning and which indicates that the expected output or response is shown, combined with the input information. The algorithm learns to forecast the suitable output based on the properties of the input parameters. Uncategorized information is trained using unsupervised learning ALGMs and is tasked with learning information PATs and structure. In reinforcement learning, an agent studies how to perform in a specified environment to increase a reward signal. ML is applied in a diversity of APLs like natural language processing, systematic analytics, detection of fraud, self-directed vehicles, image and audio identification and recommendation systems. There have been many recent advancements in the ML field that can be beneficial in efficiently MG the environment (Sarker, 2021a; Shalu, 2023).

In general, ML solution effectiveness and efficiency depend on the information characteristics and nature and the learning algorithm performance. In the area of ML ALGMs, regression, information clustering, classification study, feature engineering, and dimensionality decrease, association rule learning, or reinforcement learning approaches must exist to efficiently build information-driven systems (Sarker, 2021b).

3.5 Categories of Real-World Information

Generally, information accessibility is considered key to constructing an ML model or information-driven real-world systems. Information can be of different forms, such as semi-structured or unstructured and structured. In addition, the metadata is another category that generally represents information about the information. In the information structured form, it has a well-defined structure, which follows an information model following a typical order, which is extremely organized and effortlessly accessed and applied by an entity or a computer program. Structured information is generally stored in a well-defined system, like a relational information source in a tabular setup (Sarker, 2021a; Surur et al., 2025).

Examples of structured information are dates, stock information, geolocation, names, addresses, credit card numbers, etc. In an unstructured information form, there is no pre-defined setup or organization for unstructured information, generally encompassing text and multimedia material, making it much more problematic to capture, process, and examine. Considered examples of unstructured information include emails, blog entries, wikis and word processing documents, sensor information, audio and PDF files, images, videos, web pages and various other categories of business documents. In a semi-structured information form, information is not stored in a relational information source, such as the structured information stated directly above, but it does have certain organizational properties that make it easier to examine. Examples of semi-structured information forms are XML, JSON documents, HTML, NoSQL, etc. Metadata is not a normal form of information, but "information about information". The key variance between metadata and data is that data are simply the material that can be categorized, assessed, or even the documentation of something relative to an organization's information properties. For metadata, it defines the related data information, giving it more meaning for information handlers. A simple instance of a document's metadata is the author, information produced by the document, the size of the file, keywords to define the document, etc.

Examples of various extensively applied information sets for various purposes by researchers in the area of ML and data science include smartphone information sets – SMS, phone call, mobile application usages, and mobile phone notification logs; cybersecurity information sets – UNSW-NB15, ISCX 12, Bot-IoT, NSL-KDD, CICDDoS2019, etc; IoT information, agriculture, and e-commerce information; health information – heart disease, diabetes mellitus, COVID-19, etc and several more in different application fields. In the real world, the various information types discussed directly above may differ from application to application. To examine such information in a certain problem field, and for insights extraction from the information for building the real-world intelligent uses, various categories of ML approaches can be applied according to their learning capacity (Mahadevkar, Patil, Kotecha, Soong, & Choudhury, 2024; Sarker, 2021b).

3.5.1 Imaging from Satellite and Sensing Remotely

A comprehensive assessment of the ecological variations, like glacial melt and forest loss, is provided by satellite imaging. Critical information, such as soil moisture and temperature, is captured using remote sensing and supports in detecting the first signs of disasters and MG bionetwork health (Oliveira et al., 2024; Sand Technologies, 2023).

3.5.2 IoT Sensors and Instantaneous Tracking

Air, water, and wildlife are observed in real-time using IoT sensors, offering instantaneous information on ecological variations. These sensors assist in tracking the levels of CTN, the migration of wildlife, and provide understanding during events such as industrial and flood accidents (Sand Technologies, 2023; Ullo & Sinha, 2020).

3.5.3 Cloud Computing and Large Information Incorporation

Huge ecological information sets are stored and studied using cloud computing, guaranteeing quicker, more precise DM. By incorporating IoT and satellite information, AI-powered cloud platforms offer an instantaneous understanding of ecosystem health and potential hazards (Purnama & Sejati, 2023; Sand Technologies, 2023).

3.6 Physical World Uses of AI for Ecological Sustainability

AI is changing how organizations, conservationists and climate researchers address ecological challenges, from Latin America to Africa. Physical world examples of how AI is driving these environmental variations are discussed below (Sand Technologies, 2023).

3.6.1 MG of Air and Water Quality

The way air and soil quality is monitored has been improved by AI. In metropolises across India, AI systems process information from air sensors to observe detrimental CTN levels in real-time. This information permits authorities to issue warnings and act swiftly to guard community health (Alotaibi & Nassif, 2024; Sand Technologies, 2023).

3.6.2 Detection of Deforestation and Land Use

Serving to combat deforestation by examining satellite images and noticing prohibited logging activities is done through AI. For instance, AI tools were applied in tracking variations in the Amazon forest and observing unsanctioned land clearing. This tracking assists environmentalists in acting before substantial harm is done to the woodlands (Sand Technologies, 2023; Wang et al., 2024).

3.6.3 Conservation of Wildlife and Tracking of Species

Developing wildlife conservation by guaranteeing improved tracking of in danger of extinction species is by AI TECHs. AI-powered smart collars are applied to track rhinos in real-time in South Africa. These collars utilize AI to observe unusual activity such as potential poaching or signs of distress. The collar directs alerts via a private network to conservation teams when something seems off, thereby permitting them to respond speedily. Combined with improving safety, the collars offer a deeper understanding of Rhino behaviour and assist in shaping stronger conservation approaches (Sand Technologies, 2023).

3.7 AI Ms Limitations

In the AI domain for EMG, combined with its several benefits, there are numerous notable limitations and challenges that must be documented. An understanding of these limitations is important for the responsible and up-to-date advancement of AI Ms. A prominent limitation is information dependency, and AI Ms depend overwhelmingly on the information quality and quantity. Insufficient or prejudiced information can result in reduced model performance or algorithmic predisposition, which may disseminate discrimination. For instance, if an AI model for MG, the quality of air is trained primarily on information from built-up areas, it may not achieve well in countryside areas, leading to erroneous forecasts and possibly destructive policy decisions. A noteworthy challenge in AI modelling is overfitting, and this happens when a model learns the training information too well, leading to underprivileged generalization to fresh, unobserved information. Keeping a balance in model intricacy is central to extenuating this problem. In real-world terms, an overfitted model might precisely forecast the quality of water in certain rivers it was trained on, but fail to oversimplify to other rivers with several features (Olawade et al., 2024; Sustainability Directory, 2025).

Another puzzling challenge is the interpretability, especially in the context of DL Ms. These Ms are often defined as black boxes owing to their lack of transparency. The capacity to understand how and why an AI model attains a certain decision is central for building user trust, but it remains an unending challenge. Another constraint is resource intensiveness. Training and running intricate AI Ms demand considerable computational resources, which can be an obstruction for smaller organizations and emerging nations. This discrepancy can intensify prevailing inequalities, where only well-resourced entities can influence unconventional AI TECHs efficiently. Equally, ethical concerns are also a mounting problem in the development of AI, and they can unintentionally strengthen current prejudices existing in the training information. Guaranteeing equality and addressing ethnical concerns is a substantial challenge, especially in APLs where equality and non-discrimination are supreme. A real concern is the security threats, as AI Ms are vulnerable to aggressive attacks, were small, prudently manufactured variations to input information can deceive the model. To conclude, more evident is the environmental effect of AI Ms. Huge-scale training consumes substantial energy resources, contributing to ecological concerns (Olawade et al., 2024; Sustainability Directory, 2025).

3.8 Conclusion

ML-driven EMG systems signify a life-changing method to recognize and handle the dynamics of air, water, and soil quality. By taking advantage of unconventional ALGMs, these systems offer instantaneous, precise, and adaptive understandings of ecological settings. The integration of ML with remote sensing and BD analytics ensures the nonstop observation, analytical assessment, and proactive mitigation of ecological PLN. Yet, challenges remain in guaranteeing the information quality, model overview across various settings, and deciphering systematic outputs into actionable guidelines. Future studies should concentrate on developing hybrid and explicable ML Ms, improving cross-domain interoperability, and creating open-access ecological information frameworks. With continued invention and partnership between scientists, industries, and policymakers, ML-driven MG systems will play a fundamental part in progressing universal sustainability and resilience against ecological CTN.

References

Afoma, U., Singh, S., Mishra, A., Sharma, C., Gupta, K., Mishra, M., … Sharma, V. (2025). Integrating artificial intelligence in environmental monitoring: A paradigm shift in data-driven sustainability. *EcoHealth, 23*(1), 38–57. https://doi.org/10.1007/s10393-025-01752-8

Aigbe, U., Ukhurebor, K., Onyancha, R., Osibote, O., Darmokoesoemo, H., & Kusuma, H. (2021). Fly ash-based adsorbent for adsorption of heavy metals and dyes from aqueous solution: A review. *Journal of Materials Research and Technology, 14*, 2751–2774.

Alotaibi, E., & Nassif, N. (2024). Artificial intelligence in environmental monitoring: In-depth analysis. *Discover Artificial Intelligence, 4*(1), 84.

Bhowmick, K., Narvekar, M., & Khatkhatay, M. (2019). A comprehensive study and analysis of semi supervised learning techniques. *International Journal of Engineering Technology & Research, 8*, 810–816.

Chisom, O., Biu, P., Umoh, A., Obaedo, B., Adegbite, A., & Abatan, A. (2024). Reviewing the role of AI in environmental monitoring and conservation: A data-driven revolution for our planet. *World Journal of Advanced Research and Reviews, 21*(1), 161–171. https://doi.org/10.30574/wjarr.2024.21.1.2720

Halevi, G., Moed, H., & Bar-Ilan, J. (2017). Suitability of google scholar as a source of scientific information and as a source of data for scientific evaluation—Review of the literature. *Journal of Informetrics, 11*(3), 823–834.

Jain, H. (2024). From pollution to progress: Groundbreaking advances in clean technology unveiled. *Innovation and Green Development, 3*(2), 100143.

Jiang, T., Gradus, J., & Rosellini, A. (2020). Supervised machine learning: A brief primer. *Behavior Therapy, 51*(5), 675–687.

Kamble, A., Jiet, M., Weerarathna, I., Dhande, S., Izankar, S., & Puri, C. (2025). Reinforcement learning model, algorithms, and its application. *AIP Conference Proceedings, 3227*, 050012. AIP Publishing LLC.

Kim, Y., Park, W., Shin, Y., Park, J., Engel, B., Yun, Y., & Jang, W. (2024). Applications of machine learning and remote sensing in soil and water conservation. *Hydrology, 11*(11), 183.

Kumar, M. (2024). AI for climate change: Predicting environmental impact and developing sustainable solutions. *ESP Journal of Engineering & Technology Advancements, 4*(3), 127–133.

Li, J., Pei, Y., Zhao, S., Xiao, R., Sang, X., & Zhang, C. (2020). A review of remote sensing for environmental monitoring in China. *Remote Sensing, 12*(7), 1130.

Mahadevkar, S., Patil, S., Kotecha, K., Soong, L., & Choudhury, T. (2024). Exploring AI-driven approaches for unstructured document analysis and future horizons. *Journal of Big Data, 11*(1), 92.

Mezquita, B., Martín-Delgado, L., Wennberg-Capellades, L., & Borrego, Á. (2025). A comparison of OpenAlex with Scopus and Web of Science for tracking scholarly nursing literature. *SAGE Open Nursing, 11*, 23779608251361012.

Mohammed, M., Khan, M., & Bashier, E. (2016). *Machine learning: Algorithms and applications*. Boca Raton: CRC Press.

Ogidi, O., Onwuagba, C., & Richard-Nwachukwu, N. (2024). Biomonitoring tools, techniques and approaches for environmental assessments. In *Biomonitoring of pollutants in the global South* (pp. 243–273). Singapore: Springer Nature Singapore.

Olawade, D., Wada, O., Ige, A., Egbewole, B., Olojo, A., & Oladapo, B. (2024). Artificial intelligence in environmental monitoring: Advancements, challenges, and future directions. *Hygiene and Environmental Health Advances, 12*, 100114.

Oliveira, A., Matricardi, E., de Aragão, L., Felix, I., Chaves, J., Magliano, M., … Pereira, D. (2024). Assessing forest degradation through remote sensing in the Brazilian Amazon: Implications and perspectives for sustainable forest management. *Remote Sensing, 16*(23), 4557.

Onyancha, R., Aigbe, U., Ukhurebor, K., & Muchiri, P. (2021). Facile synthesis and applications of carbon nanotubes in heavy-metal remediation and biomedical fields: A comprehensive review. *Journal of Molecular Structure, 1238*, 130462.

Padhiary, M., Saha, D., Kumar, R., Sethi, L., & Kumar, A. (2024). Enhancing precision agriculture: A comprehensive review of machine learning and AI vision applications in all-terrain vehicle for farm automation. *Smart Agricultural Technology, 8*, 100483.

Purnama, S., & Sejati, W. (2023). Internet of things, big data, and artificial intelligence in the food and agriculture sector. *International Transactions on Artificial Intelligence, 1*(2), 156–174.

Reynolds, S., Beery, S., Burgess, N., Burgman, M., Butchart, S., Cooke, S., … Gassert, F. (2025). The potential for AI to revolutionize conservation: A horizon scan. *Trends in Ecology & Evolution, 40*(2), 191–207.

Sand Technologies. (2023, April). *AI for environmental monitoring: Benefits, uses & innovation*. Retrieved from https://www.sandtech.com/insight/ai-for-environmental-monitoring/

Sarker, I. (2021a). Data science and analytics: An overview from data-driven smart computing, decision-making and applications perspective. *SN Computer Science, 2*(5), 377.

Sarker, I. (2021b). Machine learning: Algorithms, real-world applications and research directions. *SN Computer Science, 2*(3), 160.

Sarker, I. (2022). AI-based modeling: Techniques, applications and research issues towards automation, intelligent and smart systems. *SN Computer Science, 3*(2), 158.

Shakya, K., Alavi, A., Porteous, J., Laddi, A., & Jaiswal, M. (2024). A critical analysis of deep semi-supervised learning approaches for enhanced medical image classification. *Information, 15*(5), 246.

Shalu, S. (2023). Environmental monitoring with machine learning. *EPRA International Journal of Multidisciplinary Research (IJMR), 9*(5), 208–212. https://doi.org/10.36713/epra13330

Srivastava, A., & Sharma, H. (2024). AI-driven environmental monitoring using google earth engine. In *IoT sensors, ML, AI and XAI: Empowering a smarter world* (pp. 375–385). Switzerland, Cham: Springer Nature.

Surur, F., Mamo, A., Gebresilassie, B., Mekonen, K., Golda, A., Behera, R., & Kumar, K. (2025). Unlocking the power of machine learning in big data: A scoping survey. *Data Science and Management*. *8*(4), 519–535.

Sustainability Directory. (2025, April 30). *What are the limits of AI?* Retrieved from https://pollution.sustainability-directory.com/question/what-are-the-limits-of-ai/

Sweileh, W. (2021). Bibliometric analysis of peer-reviewed literature on antimicrobial stewardship from 1990 to 2019. *Globalization and Health*, *17*(1), 1.

Taye, M. M. (2023). Understanding of machine learning with deep learning: Architectures, workflow, applications and future directions. *Computers*, *12*(5), 91.

Thenmozhi, V., & Krisknakumari, S. (2024). Artificial intelligence in enhancing operational efficiency in logistics and SCM. *International Journal of Scientific Research in Science and Technology*, *11*(5), 316–323.

Toorajipour, R., Sohrabpour, V., Nazarpour, A., Oghazi, P., & Fischl, M. (2021). Artificial intelligence in supply chain management: A systematic literature review. *Journal of Business Research*, *122*, 502–517.

Ukhurebor, K., Aigbe, U., Onyancha, R., Nwankwo, W., Osibote, O., Paumo, H., … Siloko, I. (2021). Effect of hexavalent chromium on the environment and removal techniques: A review. *Journal of Environmental Management*, *280*, 111809.

Ullo, S., & Sinha, G. (2020). Advances in smart environment monitoring systems using IoT and sensors. *Sensors*, *20*(11), 3113.

Wang, Z., Li, Z., Xie, Y., Souza, C. Jr, Souza Filho, J., & Pinheiro, S. (2024). AI-based validation of deforestation using high-resolution satellite imagery in the Brazilian Amazon. *The International Archives of the Photogrammetry, Remote Sensing and Spatial Information Sciences*, *48*, 583–588.

4

Machine Learning in Pollution Detection and Control in Air, Water, and Soil

Abstract

Machine learning (ML) application in ecological monitoring (EMG) offers precise pollution (PLN) source detection, and all-inclusive monitoring (MG) of air, soil, and water quality (QLT). This chapter offers a synopsis of the value of EMG, the challenges of traditional approaches, and potential ML-based solutions. Some substantial ML applications in EMG are emphasized, showcasing their contributions to efficient ecological administration. ML technologies (TECHs) improve EMG by aiding improved understanding, prediction, and extenuation of ecological risks. The chapter also deliberates on associated challenges like information heterogeneity, model interpretability, and the requirement for standardized information sets. Overall, ML-driven systems demonstrate substantial potential to improve ecological protection, encourage sustainability, and support data-informed policy development.

4.1 Introduction

One of the greatest threats to the health of humans and the stability of the environment in the 21st century is environmental contamination (CTN). Specifically, the quality (QLT) of air and water degradation has been directly associated with acute and chronic health issues (respiratory diseases, irritation of the skin, poisoning, nausea, vomiting, cancer, reproductive disorder, and developmental abnormalities), bionetwork interruption and socioeconomic losses. Notwithstanding the growing supervisory frameworks, CTN levels monitoring (MG) remain an intricate challenge owing to infrequent sensor coverage, information inactivity, and restricted analytical capacity. Efficient administration of harmful substances in the bionetwork needs "MG, remediation and prevention" approaches (Devender et al., 2025; Popescu et al., 2024).

Risk to human well-being, plant and animal life and the bionetwork is posed by unsafe materials in the bionetwork. These materials include "pesticides,

 DOI: 10.1201/9781003618584-4

herbicides, heavy metals (HMs) and Persistent-Organic-Pollutants (POPs)" that are introduced into the bionetwork via different means. Causes of harmful materials in the environment include industrial activities, inappropriate unsafe waste disposal, agrarian practices, and normal processes like weathering and erosion. These materials can persist in the bionetwork for extended periods and can have an undesirable effect on the QLT of soil, the growth of plants, and the health of humans. Depending on the material type and concentration, and exposure time, perilous materials' effects in the environment can differ (Popescu et al., 2024). The balance of quantity and manufacturing components price is influenced by demand and supply. CTN is understood as a key factor in productivity, and the association between ecological CTN and economic advancement in a balanced state is determined by assessing the pollution (PLN) supply and demand (Dang, Kim, Park, & Xu, 2024).

The important process of ecological monitoring (EMG) involves the methodical observation, extent, and assessment of the natural setting and all of its components. The main goal is to monitor the current settings of the environment and recognize variations that can be detrimental to the bionetwork or community health (Olawade et al., 2024). The smart TECHs trend is changing how PLN is monitored and managed (Jerome Workman, 2025). The nonstop upgrading of the QLT of life is directly linked, among other factors, with the QLT of the bionetwork. This can be advanced by using unconventional equipment and technology-based intelligent MG, examination, decision-making (DM), and control systems (Zhang, Shu, Rajkumar, & Sivakumar, 2021).

The dawn of contemporary artificial intelligence (AI) approaches has the possibility to expressively change and improve computer's role in engineering and science. Big-data (BD) and AI combination has been detailed as the "Fourth Paradigm of Science" and "Fourth Industrial Revolution", and the number of applications in the chemical field is growing at an astonishing rate. A sub-field of AI that has progressed speedily in current times is machine learning (ML). At the core of the application of ML lies in numerical algorithms (ALGMs) whose performance, much like that of a scientist, enhances with training. There is a mounting structure of ML tools for creating, testing, and refining systematic models (Ms). Such approaches are suitable for addressing intricate issues that consist of immense combinatorial spaces or non-linear processes, which traditional processes either cannot solve or can tackle only at prodigious computational expense (Butler, Davies, Cartwright, Isayev, & Walsh, 2018; Jain et al., 2013). AI emergence is increasingly shaping an array of sectors, and it is projected to influence international productivity, equality and inclusion, ecological results and other sectors, both in the short-term and long-term. It is reported that probable AI impacts show both negative and positive influences on sustainable growth (Vinuesa et al., 2020).

The convergence of ML and AI with environmental-sciences has led to substantial development in EMG and information analysis in recent years. These TECHs offer authoritative tools in addressing intricate ecological tasks by allowing more precise prediction, instantaneous MG, and the capability to analyse huge data sets that conventional approaches cannot accomplish resourcefully (Alotaibi & Nassif, 2024). AI has been developed as a vital incorporation in EMG purposes, in the quest to improve the results' objectivity and enhance availability to areas deprived of inadequate resources. It is a sub-field of computer-science, which prominences emphasis on producing ALGMs and computer programs (CPs) that can achieve activities such as learning, sensing, reasoning, and DM that would normally need human intelligence. Huge information sets can be analysed by applying AI, which has been established to be suitable for pattern identification and making specific forecasts. In EMG, it has been used in different areas such as natural disaster forecasting, air and water QLT MG and contaminants recognition. Table 4.1 gives a comparative study of AI approaches against conventional methods in terms of scalability, speed, information incorporation, precision, maintenance, and ecological effect. The substantial benefits of AI in improving the competence and usefulness of EMG are underscored by AI and while considering the possible opening costs and the position of considering long-standing advantages (Olawade et al., 2024; Srivastava & Sharma, 2024). In current times, environmental phenomena modelling and predicting, applying AI technology have surged owing to its capacity to solve practical issues associated with MG of river QLT, sewage treatment, and water resources management (Safder, Kim, Pak, Rhee, & You, 2022).

This book's interest in ML applications in the detection and control of contamination in air, water, and soil has significantly improved in modern times, and there is a requirement to have a diverse look into these thrust areas. Diverse scientific literature is included within the science field and is recognized across numerous catalogues such as "PubMed, Microsoft Academic Web of Science, Dimensions, Scopus and Google Scholar". Scopus was selected by the authors of this book to be applied, owing to its all-inclusive peer reviewed research journals and citations in this field from several international journals (Halevi, Moed, & Bar-Ilan, 2017; Mezquita, Martín-Delgado, Wennberg-Capellades, & Borrego, 2025; Padhiary, Saha, Kumar, Sethi, & Kumar, 2024).

Scopus information base is 100% all-encompassing of PubMed and is maintained by Elsevier. It consists of twice the number of journal catalogues in the WOS (Sweileh, 2021). To track academic literature and to establish the influence of publication in relation to citations, bibliographic information bases are utilized by researchers (Mezquita et al., 2025). A bibliometric study was implemented in VOSviewer using the methodology of (Padhiary et al., 2024). Based on the VOSviewer map produced from Scopus for research publications between 2015 and November 2025, it is apparent that the study landscape of ML applications in PLN detection is a highly incorporated network of different, diverse, but interwoven clusters, as shown in Figure 4.1. The term ML is the most densely connected node and the largest, which demonstrates that it is a key driver of technology across multiple clusters.

TABLE 4.1

AI Approaches Set against Outmoded Methods in EMG

Measures	AI Approaches (Detailed Model/Tool)	Outmoded Approaches
Precision	DL Ms (CNNs): High accuracy in the recognition of images and patterns (PATs) Random Forests: Efficient for handling huge information sets and recognizing multifaceted PATs "Support Vector Machines (SVMs)": Outstanding for cataloguing responsibilities	Variable precision is reliant on human know-how Vulnerable to human mistakes and biases Regularly restricted by the resolution and frequency of physical sampling (SMLG)
Speed	"Instantaneous Information Processing (TensorFlow and Keras)": Instantaneous examination and anomaly recognition Automatic MG Systems (IBM Watson): Quicker information combination and synthesis from numerous sources	Time-intensive information gathering and examination Deferred results owing to prolonged laboratory-processes Sluggish response-time in emergency circumstances
Cost	Preliminary setup can be exclusive (software, equipment, and training) Longstanding working costs are lower owing to computerization and the condensed requirement for human labour Scalable with declining marginal budgets	Highly elevated continuing costs for labour, paraphernalia, and consumables Exclusive physical SMLG and laboratory studies Expenses rise correspondingly with the measure of MG efforts
Scalability	Cloud-based platforms (Microsoft Azure and Google Cloud AI): Simply scalable to cover huge geographic zones Accomplished by incorporating information from several sources, like satellites and IoT devices	Inadequate scalability owing to dependence on human labour and physical SMLG Exclusive and logistically thought-provoking to enlarge coverage
Information Incorporation	BD Analytics Tools like Hadoop and Apache Spark: Handle and incorporate large volumes of diverse data Accomplished continuous MG and instantaneous updates	Restricted capacity to incorporate various information sources Physical information entry and slower information updates
Maintenance	Needs intermittent software updates and infrequent hardware maintenance Lesser maintenance costs over time	Systematic equipment maintenance and calibration Elevated unending costs for consumables and replacements
Ecological Effect	Lesser ecological impact owing to condensed requirement for manual SMLG and travel Energy-effective solutions, such as AI-powered sensors, lessen the carbon-footprint	Higher ecological impact from recurrent manual SMLG Travel and transportation rise carbon-footprint

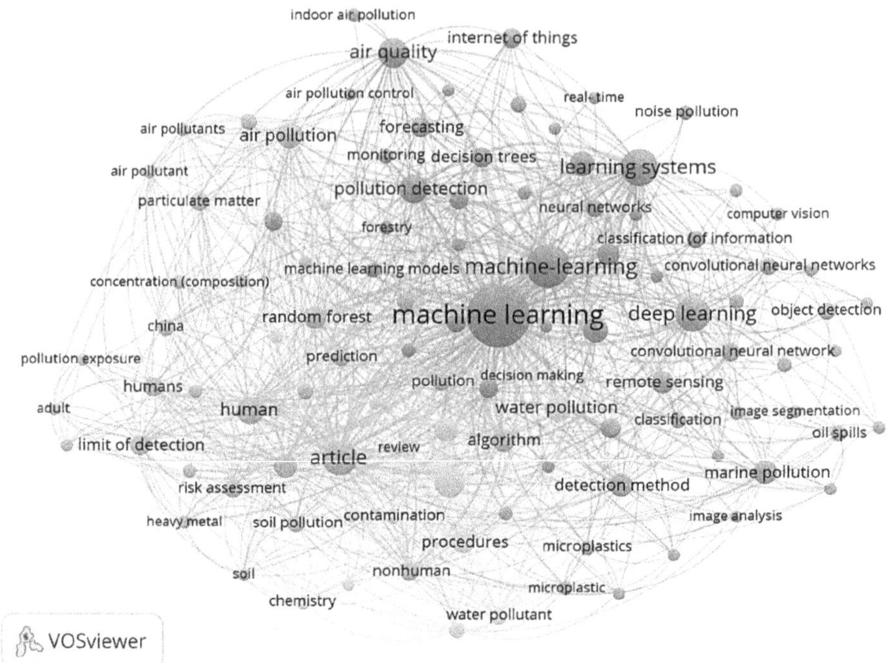

FIGURE 4.1
The keyword network diagram is based on 2024 journal articles retrieved from the Scopus catalogue with the keyword "ML and PLN Detection".

From the primary red/orange clusters, it is evident that AI, with strong use of deep-learning (DL) and convolutional neural networks (CNNs), is directly applied to PLN detection, real-time MG, and forecasting of environmental conditions, as shown in Figure 4.1. It is essential to note that the central core is connected to three primary environmental application areas. Air QLT with the green cluster shows how ML Ms are linked to air PLN and are employed for risk assessment associated with humans and other contaminants, like HMs. Marine or water PLN, shown with blue and yellow clusters, shows how the application has been extended to aquatic ecosystems to detect marine PLN and oil spills using techniques such as image segmentation and remote sensing. The yellow cluster connects ML to the detection and analysis of specific contaminants like microplastics and water pollutants. Overall, this demonstrates how ML has been utilized beyond the simple detection to involve real-time forecasting and risk assessment across air, water, and soil environments. There was an upward trend in the number of publications that were indexed in Scopus from 2015 to November 2025, based on the keywords used for search (ML and PLN detection). There was a noticeable increase in the number of articles published from 2015 November 2025 (Figure 4.2).

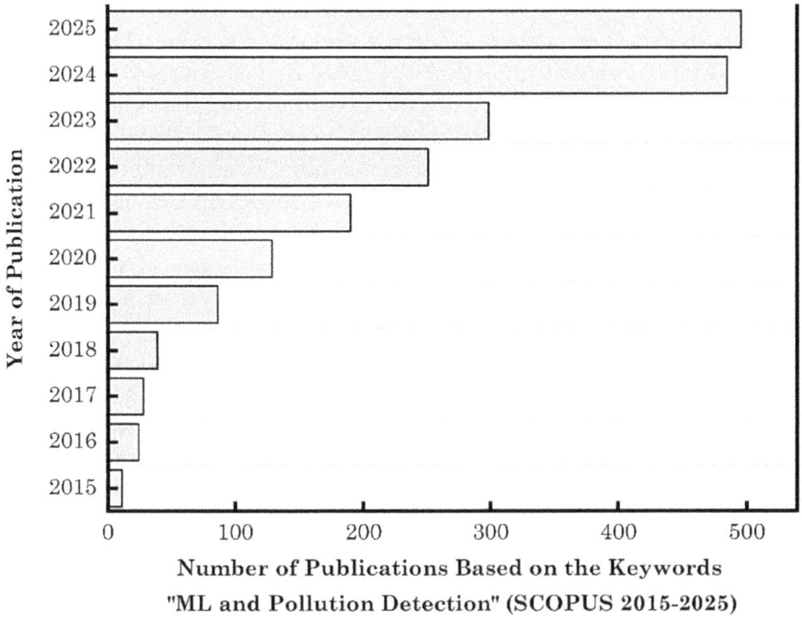

FIGURE 4.2
Scientific publications trend in the Scopus information base on ML for PLN detection from 2015 to November 2025.

4.2 AI Models for Ecological Monitoring

When selecting an AI Ms for EMG, it is vital to consider factors like availability of data, expertize and computational-resources. Some AI Ms need huge volumes of information and computational-rules to train, while others can be trained on reduced information sets with a lesser amount of computational cost (Bolón-Canedo, Morán-Fernández, Cancela, & Alonso-Betanzos, 2024; Greif, Röckel, Kimmig, & Ovtcharova, 2025; Olawade et al., 2024; Vinuesa et al., 2020). SVMs are well matched for managing high-dimensional information and learning intricate associations between variables. They can be utilized with different information types, including text and images. For example, SVMs have been applied efficiently for image cataloguing responsibilities like deforestation detection and wildlife identification. Also, to extract data from ecological reports, they are utilized in natural language (NL) processing. For regression issues in EMG, the SV Regression (SVR), a different SVM, is applied, and it offers an efficient solution for forecasting ecological control parameters (Guido, Ferrisi, Lofaro, & Conforti, 2024; Olawade et al., 2024; Sarker, 2021).

A decision-tree (DT) is a non-parametric supervised learning (SL) method that is utilized for classification and regression tasks (Sarker, 2021). DT-based

ALGMs have been used in various applications, consisting of but not restricted to regression, feature selection and classification. The simple idea behind a DT-based algorithm is that it repeatedly partitions information into subgroups based on the diverse attribute values until a stopping-condition is met. This procedure results in a tree-like structure, where an individual node indicates a decision or a split built on a detailed characteristic. The ideal attribute to apply for individual split based on certain criteria like ratio of gain, data gain and Gini index, is determined by the algorithm. They are also known for their interpretability, and the ensuing tree structure permits users to comprehend and understand the DM process effortlessly (Mienye & Jere, 2024).

DTs are moderately modest to train and understand, making them available for several categories of information. They are generally employed for tasks such as deforestation detection and MG, and air and water QLT MG. However, they can be susceptible to overfitting (OFG), particularly when managing intricate, noisy information and may not perform well on the recognition of images or NL processing responsibilities (Olawade et al., 2024). Well-known DT ALGMs are C4.5, CART and ID3. The most popular conditions for splitting are Gini for the Gini-impurity and entropy for the data gain, which can be stated scientifically by Equations 4.1 and 4.2 (Sarker, 2021).

$$Gini(E) = 1 - \sum_{i=1}^{c} Pi^2 \tag{4.1}$$

$$Entropy\text{: } H(x) = -\sum_{i=1}^{n} p(x_i)\log_2 p(x_i) \tag{4.2}$$

Proposed by Breiman in 2001 is the random forest (RF), which is a cataloguing algorithm and is hinge on the bagging idea. It blends several feeble classifiers (DTs) to create a sturdier classifier (Lan, Hu, Jiang, Yang, & Zhao, 2020). RFs are a collaborative learning approach that blends the forecasts of several DTs. They are more robust to OFG than distinct DTs and can handle/manage several information forms, as well as text and images. They are generally employed for the classification of images, processing of NL and forecasting of time series tasks in EMG. They are an ensemble-learning approach (ELA) that blends the forecasts of several trees. They are more resistant to OFG than distinct DTs and can handle different information forms, including text and images. RFs are generally applied for the classification of images, processing of NL and time series predicting tasks in EMG. Notwithstanding their sturdiness, RFs can be computationally in-depth and need significant memory and processing power (Lan et al., 2020; Olawade et al., 2024).

The CNN or ConvNet is a general discriminative DL framework that studies directly from the input without the human feature extraction requirement (Sarker, 2021). An extensively applied structure in DL, which is classic, is CNN. According to Sarker, (2021), it was first proposed by LeGun et al. in 1998 and has gained prime of life in applications and is capable of recognizing text, facial recognition, and classification of images and medical images. The amount of neural network (NN) parameters and the network complexity can be efficiently decreased by the local-connection, weight sharing, and pooling operation of CNN and therefore give a certain degree of invariance to translation misrepresentation and scaling and enabling easy-training and optimization (Rawat & Wang, 2017). Classification and training are programmed and do not need artificial-determination of which parameters to extract or the value of the feature of the image to extract before the training phase. CNN can robotically and effectively extract sophisticated abstract features to simplify the organization of images and improve the accuracy of categorization. It generally includes an input layer, a hidden layer consisting of one or more convolutional layers, pooling layers and fully linked layers and an output layer as displayed in Figure 4.3. CNN can get the network output value through the forward propagation. Through backpropagation (BPN), the weight of an individual layer can be adjusted according to error to realize the adaptive-learning and training network process. CNN also applies a drop-out that deals with the issue of OFG, which may happen in a conventional network (Lan et al., 2020; Sarker, 2021). Well matched for image cataloguing and tasks involving three-dimensional (3-D) information are CNNs. They can study intricate PATs from images short of precise programming, making them perfect for observing deforestation and the identification of wildlife. But they can be expensive to train computationally and need huge volumes of labelled information. Training CNN Ms can be thought-provoking owing to the non-existence of annotated information sets for visual identification. Pre-training model applying information from comparable fields can moderate this problem (Ayrey & Hayes, 2018; Olawade et al., 2024; Ukoba, Onisuru, Jen, Madyira, & Olatunji, 2025). Various alternatives exist that can be used in different application domains according to their learning competencies, such as ResNetXception, Visual Geometry Group (VGG), Inception, AlexNet, and so on (Sarker, 2021; Swapna, Sharma, & Prasadh, 2020).

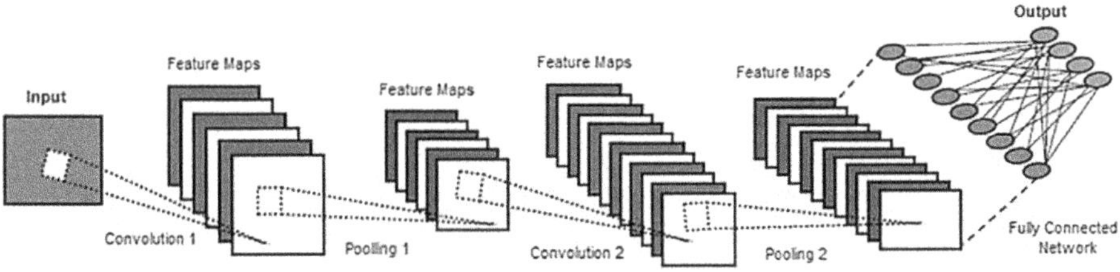

FIGURE 4.3
An illustration of a CNN or ConvNet and multiple convolution and pooling-layers. (From Sarker (2021), Springer Nature. With Permission.)

Recurrent NN is another prevalent NN, which uses chronological or time series information and feeds the outputs from the preceding stage as input to the current stage. Like the feedforward and CNN, RNs learns from the training input, but are differentiated by their memory, which permits them to influence existing input and output by applying information from preceding inputs. A distinct characteristic of deep NN (DNN) is that the inputs and outputs are independent of one another; the RNN output is dependent on the before elements within the classification. But typical RNs have a vanishing gradients issue, which makes learning long information classifications thought-provoking (Sarker, 2021). RNNs are appropriate for responsibilities involving consecutive information, like time-series prediction and NL processing. RNNs can study long-standing dependencies in information, making them efficient for forecasting exciting weather actions and extracting data from ecological reports. But, RNNs can be computationally exclusive to train and involve huge information. Cutting-edge Ms such as Convolutional Deep Long Short-Term Memory (CDLSTM) were created for more precise prediction of change in climate and change in groundwater storage modelling (Mienye, Swart, & Obaido, 2024; Olawade et al., 2024). Hybrid Ms blend the strong points of ML and DL Ms, offering high precision and robustness. They are applied for EMG tasks that need capturing intricate nonlinear (NL) interactions between input-variables and output-variables. While they can be more intricate to train and read, they provide greater performance for outstanding stakes in EMG tasks (Olawade et al., 2024; Zhao et al., 2024).

4.3 AI Models Principles

Supported by established guiding principles that form the emerging intelligence systems foundation is the AI-modelling. These ideologies offer a road-map for the production of AIMs that can tackle complex issues, systematize tasks, and make well-versed decisions. The principle of information-driven learning is central and is relied upon by AI-modelling, and the fundamental role of information in AI modelling cannot be overemphasized. AI Ms can learn from wide-ranging information sets, scrutinizing through information to distinguish trends, PATs, and associations. For instance, in the MG of air QLT, information is examined by AI Ms from different sensors to forecast CTN stages and recognize the source of CTN, as confirmed by the Synthetic Minority Over-SMLG Technique with DNN (SMOTEDNN) model for the prediction of air CTN and air QLT index (AQI) cataloguing. In another circumstance, water QLT parameters analysis (turbidity, nitrate level, and pH) is monitored using AIMs, to forecast events of PLN and to guarantee innocuous drinking water.

ML and DL ALGMs are prominent in this respect, as they harness the power of information to make forecasts and decisions (Dwivedi et al., 2023; Olawade et al., 2024).

Another fundamental AI-modelling principle is generalization. It suggests that AI Ms must be able to include their learning from certain information sets to make forecasts or decisions in a comprehensive setting. This flexibility makes sure that these Ms can manage novel, unobserved information efficiently, and this principle's practical application can be realized in the Convolutional Deep Long Short-Term Memory (CDLSTM) model, which takes a broad view from past climate information to predict future change in climate, hence assisting in EMG and DM. Also, feature engineering is a central practice that highlights the requirement for choosing applicable features or variables from the information. Meaningful input features are demanded by AI Ms to make precise forecasts. This comprises of information pre-processing, selection and transformation of features to advance the performance of the model (Dong & Liu, 2018; Olawade et al., 2024).

Hugely important is a subtle balance between model intricacy and simplicity. AI Ms must neither be too intricate nor too basic. Excessively intricate Ms can lead to OFG, where they perform remarkably well on information training, but flop to oversimplify to fresh information. On the other hand, excessively basic Ms may not capture complex PATs in the information. In training, attaining this balance can be noticed in EMG Ms that apply RFs, where ensemble approaches assist in side-stepping OFG while upholding robustness in forecasts. Furthermore, these Ms should observe the non-stop learning principle. They should be considered to acclimatize and advance over time, learning from fresh information to enhance their significance and performance. In conclusion, of supreme standing is the interpretability of the model. Considering how and why an AI-model reaches a detailed decision is central for user-trust and addressing ethical-concerns. In the background of EMG, an interpretable model supports stakeholders in understanding the features contributing to CTN, hence enabling policy development and informed DM (Khanam, Hussain, Hill, & Allen, 2024; Olawade et al., 2024).

With the swift advancement of AI, ML is increasingly playing a central role in dealing with very huge information sets. So far, regularly utilized ML ALGMs are SL ALGMs like "artificial neural networks (ANN), Random Forest (RF) and SVM". These are generally pivot on model information for computer modelling for regression and classification. A direct association between the information and the weakness of the effect of outliers can be established by ML Ms, offering sophisticated forecast precision and robustness when dealing with huge information sets. An improved fit to the information with a reduced root mean square error (RMSE) is produced by ML, especially in NL conditions. When constructing a model, multiple information types, such as integers and strings, can be introduced. When compared to numerical Ms, ML Ms are comparatively modest, less laborious, and low priced. These advantages make the ML model ever more prevalent in environmental PLN science studies. Furthermore, several categories of information, such as strings and integers, can be introduced into the model structure. ML Ms are comparatively modest, reasonable, and less time-consuming when compared to numerical Ms. These benefits make ML Ms progressively common in atmospheric science exploration. Blended with numerous fields of information, these ML Ms are important components for many tasks like instant predicting, scrutiny of the chemical behaviour of contaminants, and impact valuation (Li, Sha, Tang, Goulding, & Liu, 2023).

4.4 Real-World Setups of AI in Environmental Monitoring

This book segment will feature the real-world cases of AI (ML) being applied to monitor and guard the health and well-being of the bionetwork. AI and ML use in EMG has seen substantial diversification and development. These TECHs have been used in different fields to address key ecological problems, representing their resourcefulness and efficiency (Alotaibi & Nassif, 2024). AI is supporting humans to monitor and save our Earth in various novel ways. These smart tools let us recognize and care for the earth better than before. A key way that AI assists is by observing the bionetwork. AI can crisscross tons of information from various spots, such as space and things on the ground. Based on this information, what is going on within our air, water and soil is revealed (Islam, 2025).

4.4.1 Monitoring of Air Quality

A substantial natural problem that affects the QLT of life, community health, and economic advancement is the CTN of air. It is an intricate blend of different gases and particles created from both human activities (emissions from vehicles, processes from industries, and fossil fuel burning) and natural sources (volcanic eruptions and wildfires). These contaminants degrade the air QLT that we inhale, but also contribute to an array of health issues (Chen et al., 2024). The atmosphere comprises of several invisible and elusive contaminants. Contaminants in the air are substances that exist in the atmosphere and can have different adverse effects on the health of human and the environment. They can occur as solid particles, liquid droplets, or gases, frequently in aerosol form (liquid droplets or solid particles). They are generally grouped into primary and secondary contaminants, with the primary contaminants directly released from sources like fossil fuels and volcanic ash (these contaminants are harmful to the point of emission, and common primary contaminants consist of sulphur dioxide (SO_2) – burning of fossil fuel such as coal and oil; carbon dioxide (CO) – vehicle exhaust and emission from industries; nitrogen oxide (NO_2) – industrial and transportation activities; particulate matter (PM) – consist of PM_{10} and PM_{25}, which originate from vehicle exhaust, dust from construction sites, and emission from industries and volatile organic compounds (VOCs) emitted from solvent application, production of chemicals, and paints). The secondary contaminants are created in the atmosphere via chemical reaction, consisting of primary contaminants that are released directly (common secondary contaminants consist of ozone (O_3) created by photochemical reaction between NO_2 and VOCs in the presence of sunlight; sulphates and nitrate (SN) created from SO_2 and NO_2 in the atmosphere; and photochemical smog (PA) – an intricate blend of contaminants created via photochemical reactions comprising of O_3, peroxyacetyl nitrate (PAN) and other oxidants). Concise in Figure 4.4 are the details of the primary and secondary contaminants in the air (NIEHS, 2025; Zhang, 2025).

Contaminants continue to be restricted to their source areas and can be transported over long distances by weather and wind PATs. For illustration, inner-city contaminants can travel to countryside areas, exacerbating the air QLT problem there. The geophysical site of CTN sources plays a central part in this process. Industrial precincts positioned upwind of suburban areas can substantially affect the QLT of air downwind. Also, countryside contaminants can be carried into inner-city areas, especially during particular weather settings like temperature inversions, which confine contaminants close to the ground. The cross-provincial transmission of contaminants complicates efforts to manage the QLT of air and requires coordinated policies and measures across various areas (Zhang, 2025).

In the neighbourhood and internationally, this type of PLN negatively impacts health, contributing to severe circumstances such as respiratory

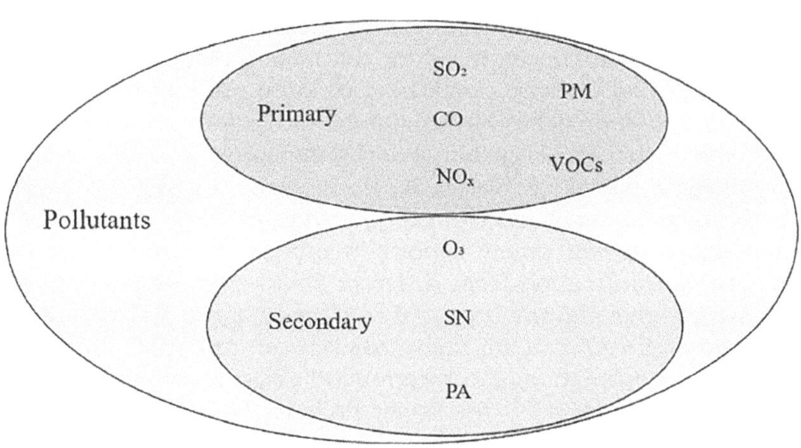

FIGURE 4.4
Different types of contaminants in the air. (From Zhang (2025), Springer Nature. With Permission.)

disorders, cancer, and cardiovascular ailments (Manisalidis, Stavropoulou, Stavropoulos, & Bezirtzoglou, 2020; Olawade et al., 2024). The old, children and those with pre-existing health circumstances are predominantly susceptible to these hostile effects. As urbanization and industrialization continue to grow, the air CTN problem becomes more unrelenting, making it an issue of principal importance for scientists, policymakers and the wider community alike. Furthermore, the PLN of the air also substantially influences changes in climate, impacting both global temperatures and the pattern of weather. This inter-connection between the QLT of air and climatic systems underscores the urgency of incorporating control of air CTN in a larger ecological policy. Also, the costs linked with the PLN of the air are overwhelming, encompassing health expenses for treating ailments caused by contaminated air and loss of employment productivity owing to sickness. Ground-breaking solutions that extend policy changes, technological progressions in emission control, and improved public awareness are required to address these problems (Atuyambe et al., 2024; Chen et al., 2024). To address this problem, there has been an amplified attention on applying AI for MG to the QLT of air. AI-powered systems can deliver accurate, real-time information on the QLT of air, supporting the established order in producing effective guidelines and interventions to reduce air CTN (Olawade et al., 2024).

A central area where AI and ML have shown substantial promise is in the MG of the QLT of air. The levels of air QLT are monitored using AI and ML approaches. For example, ML Ms can examine past information on air CTN and meteorological variables to predict future levels of CTN. This data is central for community health planning and policy making. High precision of air QLT forecasts can be achieved by applying NNs and ELA (Alotaibi & Nassif, 2024). Conventional air QLT MG systems rely on fixed sensors that provide information at certain sites; hence, these systems often lack the 3-D and time-based resolution required for complete ecological evaluations. To improve the QLT of air monitored, by providing more precise and timely forecasts, AI/ML approaches have the potential to incorporate information from different sources like sensor networks, meteorological information and satellite imagery (Alotaibi & Nassif, 2024).

AI-based recommendations can guide responses when the QLT of air is hindered, guaranteeing timely actions to protect community health. ML ALGMs assess information from different sources, encompassing sensors for air QLT, weather information, and satellite imaging, to provide instantaneous data on the QLT of air. These ALGMs can recognize the sources of CTN, CTN level estimation, and recommend possible actions to reduce air CTN by learning to identify trends and PATs in the information. In recent years, the generally used AI ALGMs for the analysis and forecast of the QLT of air are ANN, Deep Neural Networks (DNN), SVM, and fuzzy logic. But AI model choice generally is contingent on the needed data and the nature of air contaminants in the area (Olawade et al., 2024).

4.4.2 Monitoring Water Quality

MG water QLT is another key ecological field, where AI and ML have shown substantial value. To evaluate and forecast, the QLT of water parameters like dissolved oxygen (DO), pollutant levels, and pH, AI-driven Ms are used. Real-time evaluations that are central for managing water resources and guaranteeing beneficial, cleaner water are provided by Ms which can process information from sensor networks and remote sensing TECHs. Conventional assessment of the QLT of water depends on physical SMLG and laboratory analysis, which can be time-consuming, exclusive, and logistically stimulating, especially in inaccessible areas. AI/ML approaches give the potential to automate and improve these processes by using information from the sensor systems, remote sensing platforms, and past information sources to forecast the parameters of water QLT in real time (Alotaibi & Nassif, 2024).

Our water can be prudently studied using AI. The level of acid, how clear it is, and the quantity of oxygen for marine life are checked using AI. This assists in determining if water is fit for both bionetwork and human use. By researching past information, AI can even forecast whether our water will be contaminated or clean in the upcoming years. This forethought permits us to take pre-emptive steps to halt CTN before it happens. Also, AI assists in noticing breaks in water-carrying pipes. AI can recognize possible leaks by MG the flow PATs of water. This allows timely maintenance and assists in conserving water resources. This can make our water cleaner at the places where it is treated. These plants utilize chemical and energy to ensure that the drinkable water is safe. This makes the cleaning process of water work better and can save energy and money. So, AI assist us in accomplishing clean drinking water in a smarter way (Islam, 2025).

4.4.3 Change in Climate Modelling

AI/ML approaches have progressively been used in the modelling of change in climate and forecasting, where conventional replication Ms often struggle with the intricacy and scale of ecological information. ML ALGMs are influential in modelling the change in climate, where they are applied to simulate and forecast PATs of climate that hinge on large-scale ecological information. These Ms assist in acknowledging the effects of the change in climate and in advancing approaches for justification and adaptation (Alotaibi & Nassif, 2024). ML offers a powerful tool for uncovering PATs and making predictions based on a huge quantity of past climatic information, enabling more precise predictions of the impacts of climate change and well-informed DM for justification and adaptation approaches (Alotaibi & Nassif, 2024).

For the whole planet, AI is like a weather tracker. Information from satellites is applied to see how the ocean's surface is heating up or cooling down. AI assists in understanding how our climate is ever-changing, and this data is crucial for scientists and assisting in knowing what to expect in the coming years. AI performs like a fantastic smart computer that can guess what our imminent climate will be like. Based on the lots of information given by scientists about the Earth's weather works, this information can be used by AI to make various conceivable pictures of what might arise with things such as temperature and rain in the coming years. This assists scientists in understanding how the change in climate will impact us and plan what we can do to make things better. Future climate conditions are produced by AI-powered CPs. These programs will assist scientists to learn how the change in climate might impact things. Due to this, scientists can plan ways to decrease the bad effects of the change in climate (Islam, 2025).

4.4.4 Monitoring of Soil Contamination

One of the determinants of agricultural productivity is soil, and its health determines food yield, QLT, and production. To make sure that the soil has the fertility to support crop cycles, soil sustainable management needs a correct examination (Kumar et al., 2024). A significant development in agricultural management, ecological conservation, and land use planning is represented by AI application in soil MG. Conventional MG of soil approaches, which comprises of labour-intensive SMLG and laboratory study, are often laborious, labour-intensive, and restricted in scope. AI, however, offers innovative solutions that improve precision, scalability, and effectiveness, transforming how the health of soil is observed and managed. ML ALGMs like RF and DTs have proven to be predominantly efficient in handling intricate information sets with several variables. These ALGMs forecast soil properties such as the level of nutrients, pH, and moisture content by examining a huge volume of information from different sources (Awais et al., 2023; Olawade et al., 2024). There is authenticated SL in some ALGMs for soil QLT parameters assessment for regression and classification. For example, such ALGMs comprise of RF, SVM, and the Gradient Boosting Tree (GBT). These can be applied to a huge amount of information resulting from the soil factors like pH, levels of nutrients, and organic matter to forecast PATs underlying those that can forecast the QLT of soil harmoniously. This has essentially been effective in soil attributes containing factors such as organic matter, nutrient levels, and pH prediction via SL-based ML ALGMs (Kumar et al., 2024; TavallaieNejad, Vila, Paneiro, & Baptista, 2025; Vij & Prashant, 2024).

4.5 ML Models in Ecological Monitoring

Amongst the most extensively employed ML Ms, SVMs shine in categorizing the QLT of water and air by processing meteorological and contaminant information, while the RF is highly efficient in forecasting the levels of CTN, evaluating the trend of climate and categorizing land cover changes applying satellite imagery. ML Ms applied in EMG are defined by Figure 4.5 (Afoma et al., 2025).

ANN can study intricate information and is applied for predicting extreme weather events, climate variation modelling, and ecological anomalies detection. Furthermore, DTs provide interpretable Ms for the assessment of ecological risk, while k-nearest neighbours (k-NN) are generally applied for 3-D information assessment and CTN sources identification. Gradient Boosting Machine (GBMs), which consist of XGBoost and LightGBM, are used for high-accuracy EMG tasks like forecasting greenhouse gas emissions and optimization of the energy pattern of consumption. These ML Ms give benefits like extraordinary precision, flexibility to various information sets, and the automation of EMG processes. But challenges like the requirement for huge information sets, computational intricacy, and model interpretability persist. In spite of these limitations, ML continues to revolutionize ecological science by enabling proactive DM and justifiable administration of natural resources (Afoma et al., 2025; Bamal, Uddin, & Olbert, 2024).

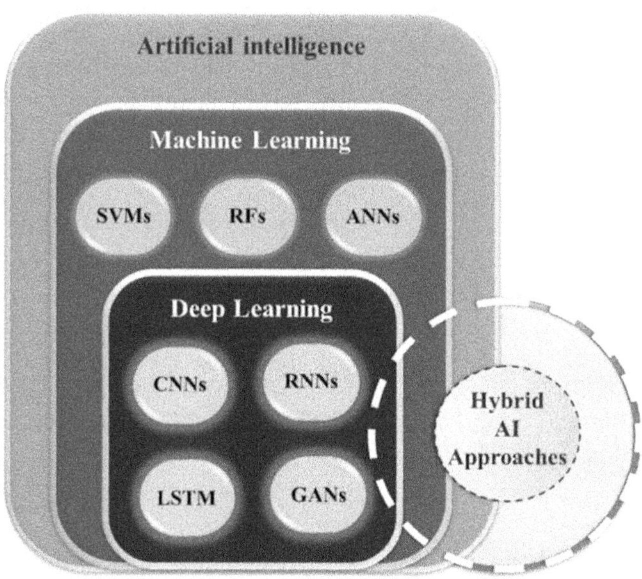

FIGURE 4.5
An AI-based model system in EMG. Demonstration of association among ML, DL, and hybrid AI Ms (blend of ML and DL methods) under the umbrella of AI: SVMs, RF, ANNs, CNNs, RNNs, LSTM, Long Short-Term Memory, and Generative Adversarial Networks (GANs). (From Afoma et al. (2025), Springer Nature. With Permission.)

4.5.1 Support Vector Machines (SVMs)

SVMs play a central part in EMG owing to their capacity to handle intricate, high-dimensional information with elevated accuracy. They are generally applied for the prediction of the QLT of air by assessing meteorological parameters and contaminants concentrations like $PM_{2.5}$, NO_2, and SO_2, assisting in categorizing the QLT of air into various CTN levels. In the evaluation of water QLT, SVM efficiently categorizes that water samples are hinge on pointers such as pH, turbidity, and DO, assisting in PLN detection in lakes, groundwater, and rivers (Afoma et al., 2025; Mogollón-Sotelo et al., 2021; Patel et al., 2025). Furthermore, SVMs support in identifying the PATs of climate and forecasting risky weather events like droughts and heat waves by assessing meteorological and satellite information. Another central use is in remote sensing and the classification of land use, where this model is applied to process satellite imagery to categorize ecological impact assessments, land cover types, and supporting biodiversity conservation. In the detection of waste and CTN, it assists in predicting the trends of the generation of waste and knowing hazardous CTN sources, optimizing recycling approaches and reducing ecological threats. The benefits of SVM in EMG comprise of its capability to handle NL association via the kernel trick, sturdiness to noisy information, and usefulness even with inadequate information sets. But, high computational expenses, the requirement for cautious factor tuning and the difficulty in interpreting SVM Ms remain the key tasks. In spite of these challenges, it continues to be an authoritative tool in ecological study, contributing to justifiable advancement and ideal resource administration. ML Ms like SVMs, DTs, and ensemble approaches allow for real-time MG and prediction of CTN from air. These systems can recognize CTN hotspots and anticipate crucial thresholds by incorporating sensor networks with predictive ALGMs (Afoma et al., 2025; Leong, Kelani, & Ahmad, 2020; Locke & Paschalidis, 2015; Riaz et al., 2024; Sedighkia & Datta, 2023). The potential of SVMs in addressing the intricacies of water QLT information sets has captured the interest of scientists. This model identifies complex PATs within the information, making it well-suited for the multifaceted nature of the QLT of water parameters such as DO, ammoniacal nitrogen (AN), BOD, COD, pH, and suspended solids (SS) (Abobakr Yahya et al., 2019; Mamat, Mohd Razali, & Hamzah, 2023; VVR, Silpa, Padmaja, Reddy, & GSLNVS, 2025).

4.5.2 Random Forest (RF)

Natural resources sustainable management is dependent on robust and evidence-based DM. A detailed evaluation of ecological factors, like the levels of pollutants, is central for recognizing hazards, designing justification approaches and assessing their usefulness (Frank, Suesse, & Brenning, 2025). RF model has proven to be successful in creating groundwater potential maps, stream flow predictions, forecasting the level of groundwater, assessing the impact of urbanization on hydrological variables, consumption prediction of urban water, forecasting of water in-rust rate in coal mines, and the rate of soil infiltration. This model is generally appropriate when NL associations exist, which is the case in mainstream water science processes. This model has also been popular in the prediction of the indicators of the QLT of water (Zavareh, Maggioni, & Zhang, 2023).

RF is a highly powered ML algorithm extensively applied in EMG owing to its ability to manage huge, intricate information sets with high robustness and precision. It is essentially efficient in the cataloguing and regression responsibilities, and this makes it suitable for different ecological uses. RF is applied in analysing meteorological and contaminants information like $PM_{2.5}$, NO_2, SO_2, CO, and O_3 to predict the level of CTN and recognize factors contributing to deprived air QLT of air (Afoma et al., 2025; Cipriano, Noce, Mereu, & Santini, 2025; Junus et al., 2025). In the evaluation of water QLT, this model assists in classifying the samples of water centred on pH, BOD, and DO parameters, thereby assisting in the early detection of PLN and its sources. It is broadly used in change in climate research, where it supports in forecasting extreme weather events, analysing temperature tendencies and evaluating the effects of worldwide warming. Furthermore, this model plays a central part in environmental MG. In the management of waste, RF is applied in recycling approach optimization, prediction of the trends of waste generation, and recognition of perilous CTN sources. The benefits of RF in EMG comprises of its capacity to handle NL associations, decrease OFG via EL and offer feature importance ranking, making it informal to interpret results. But, limitations of amplified computational intricacy and the need for huge information sets remain, and notwithstanding these restrictions, RF remains an extremely efficient tool in ecological science, contributing to information-driven DM (IDDM) for sustainable ecological management (Afoma et al., 2025; Behrouz, Yazdi, & Sample, 2022; Dewi, Wei, Lin, & Heng, 2024; Frank et al., 2025; Habeeb & Mustafa, 2025).

4.5.3 ANNs Model

Due to their capability to model intricate, NL associations and process huge information sets with elevated accuracy, ANNs are progressively applied. They are essentially efficient in extrapolative analytics and the recognition of PATs, making them suitable for numerous ecological uses. In the prediction of the QLT of air, ANNs examine contaminant and meteorological information like $PM_{2.5}$, NO_2, O_3, and CO_2 to predict CTN levels and recognize the emerging trend of CTN (Afoma et al., 2025; Cabaneros, Calautit, & Hughes, 2019; Kumar et al., 2022; Videnova, Nedialkov, Dimitrova, & Popova, 2006). For the evaluation of the QLT of water, pH, turbidity, and DO process parameters are evaluated using ANNs to categorize the QLT of water and recognize the sources of PLN (Afoma et al., 2025; Chen, Song, Liu, Yang, & Li, 2020; Gupta, Singh, & Chaudhary, 2021; Palani, Liong, & Tkalich, 2008). In the change of climate modelling, ANNs are generally used, where they assist in forecasting risky events of weather, examine temperature disparities, and evaluate longstanding trends in climate. In waste administration, they are utilized to optimize recycling processes, forecast the pattern of waste generation, and recognize illegal dumping sites. The key benefits of this model in EMG comprise of their capacity to study from large, intricate information sets, adapt to original information PATs, and provide high-precision forecasts. But their key challenges consist of the requirement for large training information sets, elevated computational expenses, and the ANN black box nature, which makes interpretation problematic. This model continues to be a valuable tool in ecological science despite these challenges, hence enabling IDDM for sustainable resource administrations (Afoma et al., 2025; Chisom et al., 2024).

4.6 Deep-Learning Models

These are subsets of ML, which have increased importance owing to their capacity to process unstructured information like images and sensor readings. They are progressively changing EMG by processing huge, intricate information sets and mining complex PATs for precise forecasts and DM, as well as these Ms being principally efficient in applications that consist of high-dimensional information like climate prediction, detection of CTN, and satellite imagery study (Afoma et al., 2025).

4.6.1 CNN Model

For CNNs, they are generally applied in land use classification, assisting in deforestation detection, remote sensing, water body changes, and urban expansion by examining satellite and aerial images. CNNs are widely applied in EMG owing to their capacity to examine 3-D and graphic information, making them especially efficient in processing information from remote sensing, imagery from satellites, and recognition of ecological PATs (Acuña-Alonso, García-Ontiyuelo, Barba-Barragáns, & Álvarez, 2024; Afoma et al., 2025; Li, 2025; Singgalen, Sutresno, Agus, & Dasra, 2025). They excel in identifying water body changes by applying high-resolution images from satellites. Aerial images and sensor information are examined to detect the source of CTN and forecast the QLT of air levels. By processing meteorological images from satellites, they are used in tracking variations in temperature, the formation of clouds, and extreme weather PATs. Furthermore, they also play a central part in the assessment of the QLT of water by recognizing CTN in water bodies via hyperspectral and multi-spectral imagery

(Afoma et al., 2025; Basit et al., 2024; Chakma, Vizena, Cao, Lin, & Zhang, 2017; Coţolan & Moldovan, 2024; Dalal, 2024; Elbaz, Shaban, Zhou, & Shen, 2023; Utku et al., 2025). Their capability to routinely extract pertinent features from images with high precision in the recognition of PATs and scalability for huge information sets are benefits of the use of CNNs. But, the requirement for extensive labelled training information, elevated computational needs, and Ms interpretability are the key challenges associated with this model. This model continues to advance EMG by providing a comprehensive understanding and improving DM for sustainable resources administration and conservation efforts. Figure 4.6 gives the different pros and cons of the use of the different Ms for EMG (Afoma et al., 2025).

4.6.2 Recurrent NNs (RNNs) and Long Short-Term Memory (LSTM)

These networks (RNNs and LSTMs) are generally applied in EMG, especially for time series predictions and sequential information study. These Ms shine at catching time-based dependencies, which makes them appropriate for forecasting ecological tendencies, examining climate distinctions and over time, MG levels of CTN (Afoma et al., 2025; Waqas & Humphries, 2024). They are generally used in the prediction of the QLT of the air, where historical sensor information is processed to predict concentrations of contaminants like $PM_{2.5}$, NO_2, CO, O_3, and SO_2, and assist in early warnings for events of air PLN (Afoma et al., 2025; Sun et al., 2022; Tsai, Zeng, & Chang, 2018; Xayasouk, Lee, & Lee, 2020; Yuan et al., 2025). They are also efficient in the modelling of climate change, examining historical temperature, humidity, and atmospheric pressure tendencies to forecast imminent PATs of climate and extreme events of weather like storms and heatwaves (Afoma et al., 2025). For the prevention of water CTN, a groundwater QLT forecast has practical significance. The LSTM RNN Ms were applied to determine the water QLT indicators based on the external variables (groundwater QLT index) such as temperature, humidity, and rate of rainfall (Valadkhan, Moghaddasi, & Mohammadinejad, 2022). Based on the LSTM model combined with other Ms simulation calculations, the forecast precision for DO, BOD, ammonia-nitrogen (NH_3-H), and pH in the prediction of the QLT of water was efficient in determining the water QLT changes (He et al., 2024; Jaffar, Thamrin, Ali, Misnan, & Yassin, 2022; Nisharga & Narmadha, 2025; Qi, Huang, & Wang, 2020; Ruan, Cui, Song, & Mao, 2023; Wongburi & Park, 2023; Zhang, Wang, Qi, & Wen, 2022). The main pros of the RNNs and LSTMs in EMG consist of their ability to learn successive dependencies, handle intricate time-based PATs, and enhanced predicting precision for active ecological systems. High computational expenses, huge training information needs, and difficulty in interpretability are key challenges that remain. Notwithstanding these challenges, these DL Ms continue to transform ecological science by ensuring initial warning systems, instantaneous MG, and IDDM for sustainable ecological administration (Afoma et al., 2025).

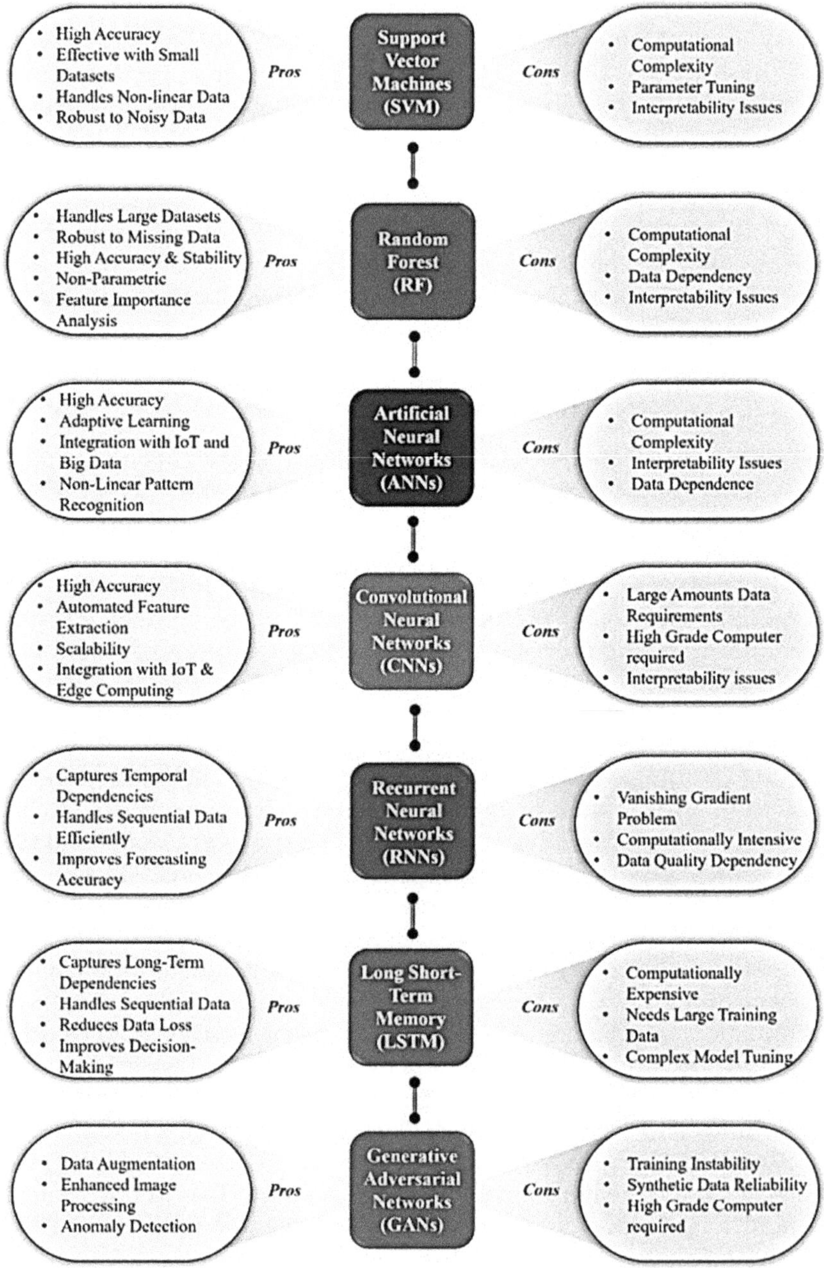

FIGURE 4.6
Benefits and disadvantages of several AI Ms used in EMG, with key evaluation of the model factors like accuracy, computational demands, information needs, interpretability, adaptability, and application scope in handling ecological information. (From Afoma et al. (2025), Springer Nature. With Permission.)

4.7 Hybrid AI Methods

Increasingly being applied in EMG to improve predictive precision, enhancing information processing, and providing better DM capabilities are hybrid AI approaches that combine several AI approaches like ML, DL, and statistical modelling. These Ms incorporate the strong points of various AI approaches, allowing for more vigorous and flexible ecological solutions. A primary use of hybrid AI is in the prediction of the QLT of air, where conventional ML Ms such as RF or SVM are blended with RNNs or LSTM networks to examine both 3-D and temporal trends of air CTN, and hence, this enhances prediction precision by capturing nonlinear associations in CTN information. Also, in the modelling of change in climate, these approaches incorporate DL with physical climate Ms to improve forecasts of temperature differences, sea level rise, and extreme events of weather. Furthermore, the blending of Internet of Things (IoT) sensor information with AI Ms improves instantaneous MG of the QLT of water, the health of the soil, and atmospheric setting by blending sensor-driven ML Ms with DL based anomaly detection. Enhanced accuracy and adaptability to various information types, and the ability to process huge-scale ecological information are the benefits of applying these approaches. Computational complications, information incorporation problems, and interpretability are challenges associated with these approaches. Yet they are proving to be transformative in ecological science, leading to initial warning systems, more effective MG and IDDM for sustainable and conservation efforts (Afoma et al., 2025).

4.7.1 Technical Challenges Related to Applying AI in Ecological Monitoring

Applying AI in EMG faces numerous technical hurdles. The intricacy of ecological systems poses a substantial challenge, as these systems are extremely dynamic and comprise of various interacting variables, making it tough for AI Ms to capture all applicable factors precisely. Another key issue is model interpretability, especially with DL Ms often defined as "black boxes". The dearth of transparency can also hamper understanding of how these Ms arrive at their forecasts, which is central for ecological DM. Furthermore, substantial computational-resources are required by AI Ms processing huge-scale ecological information, which can be a limiting factor for organizations or areas with restricted access to an extraordinary performance computing setup. Figure 4.7 shows the important facts on the challenges in applying AI for EMG (Chauhan, Vedrtnam, Wyche, & Verma, 2025)

4.7.2 Information-Associated Challenges

Existing information on QLT and accessibility are contemporary challenge in the application of AI for EMG. AI Ms need huge, extraordinary-QLT

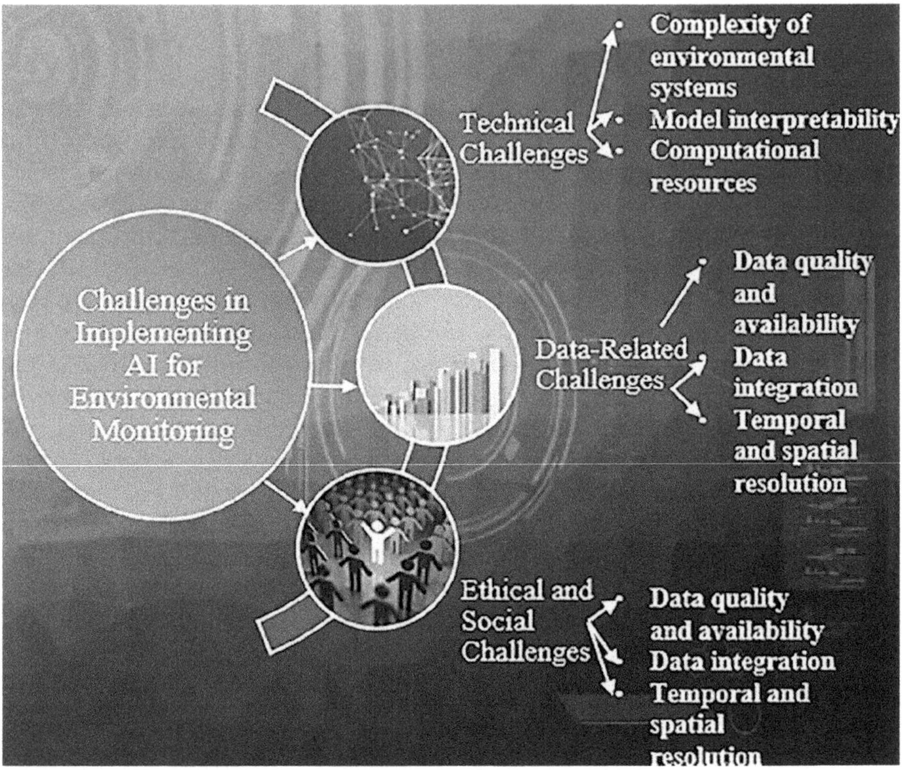

FIGURE 4.7
Challenges in applying AI for EMG. (From Chauhan et al. (2025), Springer Nature. With Permission.)

information sets for training, but ecological information can frequently be scarce, unpredictable, or of variable QLT, impacting the performance of the model. Information incorporation is another problem, as EMG encompasses several information types from numerous sources like satellite imagery, sensor networks, and citizen science. Incorporating these diverse information sources can be thought-provoking for AI systems. Also, ecological information frequently differs in spatial and temporal resolution, complicating the advancement of AI Ms that require working across various scales (Chauhan et al., 2025).

4.7.3 Ethical and Social Challenges

The application of AI in EMG also raises numerous ethical and social concerns. Privacy is an important problem, as EMG can comprise of the collection of information that may overstep on the specific privacy, specifically in built-up bionetworks. Fairness and availability present another challenge, as AI applications in EMG may not be correspondingly available for all areas or societies, possibly aggravating prevailing disparities in ecological administration and protection. Reliance and acceptance of AI-based EMG systems among shareholders, as well as policymakers and the community, are central for efficient application. To conclude, the swift advancement of AI TECHs frequently outperforms regulatory frameworks, producing challenges in governing the application of AI in EMG and policymaking (Chauhan et al., 2025).

4.8 Conclusion

In this chapter, the up-to-date applications of AI in EMG and the importance of its capability to overcome the limitations of outmoded approaches are reviewed. The incorporation of AI in EMG offers an essential advantage across different fields, such as the MG of air, soil, and water QLT. These progressions contribute substantially to the protection of the bionetwork, community health, and sustainable advancement. The capability of AI to provide detailed forecasts and instantaneous MG improves the effectiveness of ecological administration practices. Ecological information and resources can be well used by exploiting the influence of AI to preserve the well-being of our world and its populations.

References

Abobakr Yahya, A., Ahmed, A., Binti Othman, F., Ibrahim, R., Afan, H., El-Shafie, A., … Elshafie, A. (2019). Water quality prediction model based support vector machine model for ungauged river catchment under dual scenarios. *Water, 11*(6), 1231.

Acuña-Alonso, C., García-Ontiyuelo, M., Barba-Barragáns, D., & Álvarez, X. (2024). Development of a convolutional neural network to accurately detect land use and land cover. *MethodsX, 12*, 102719.

Afoma, U., Singh, S., Mishra, A., Sharma, C., Gupta, K., Mishra, M., & Sharma, V. (2025). Integrating artificial intelligence in environmental monitoring: A paradigm shift in data-driven sustainability. *EcoHealth, 23*, 38–57.

Alotaibi, E., & Nassif, N. (2024). Artificial intelligence in environmental monitoring: In-depth analysis. *Discover Artificial Intelligence, 4*(1), 84.

Atuyambe, L., Arku, R., Naidoo, N., Kapwata, T., Asante, K., Cissé, G., … Berhane, K. (2024). The health impacts of air pollution in the context of changing climate in Africa: A narrative review with recommendations for action. *Annals of Global Health, 90*(1), 76.

Awais, M., Naqvi, S., Zhang, H., Li, L., Zhang, W., Awwad, F., & Hu, J. (2023). AI and machine learning for soil analysis: An assessment of sustainable agricultural practices. *Bioresources and Bioprocessing, 10*(1), 90.

Ayrey, E., & Hayes, D. (2018). The use of three-dimensional convolutional neural networks to interpret LiDAR for forest inventory. *Remote Sensing, 10*(4), 649.

Bamal, A., Uddin, M., & Olbert, A. (2024). Harnessing machine learning for assessing climate change influences on groundwater resources: A comprehensive review. *Heliyon, 10*(17). e37073. https://doi.org/10.1016/j.heliyon.2024.e37073

Basit, M., Iqbal, M., Saleem, M., Hussain, A., Khalil, M., & Khan, M. (2024). Investigate the use of AI in environmental monitoring and prevention of avoidable hazards. *Kashf Journal of Multidisciplinary Research, 1*(11), 15–2.

Behrouz, M., Yazdi, M., & Sample, D. (2022). Using random forest, a machine learning approach to predict nitrogen, phosphorus, and sediment event mean concentrations in urban runoff. *Journal of Environmental Management, 317,* 115412.

Bolón-Canedo, V., Morán-Fernández, L., Cancela, B., & Alonso-Betanzos, A. (2024). A review of green artificial intelligence: Towards a more sustainable future. *Neurocomputing, 599,* 128096.

Butler, K., Davies, D., Cartwright, H., Isayev, O., & Walsh, A. (2018). Machine learning for molecular and materials science. *Nature, 559*(7715), 547–555.

Cabaneros, S., Calautit, J., & Hughes, B. (2019). A review of artificial neural network models for ambient air pollution prediction. *Environmental Modelling & Software, 119,* 285–304.

Chakma, A., Vizena, B., Cao, T., Lin, J., & Zhang, J. (2017). Image-based air quality analysis using deep convolutional neural network. In *2017 IEEE International Conference on Image Processing (ICIP)* (pp. 3949–3952). IEEE.

Chauhan, B., Vedrtnam, A., Wyche, K., & Verma, S. (2025). Review on artificial intelligence in the environmental monitoring. In A Vedrtnam, K. P. Wyche, B.V. S. Chauhan & S. Verma (Eds.). *Prospects of artificial intelligence in the environment* (pp. 29–60). Singapore: Springer Nature.

Chen, F., Zhang, W., Mfarrej, M., Saleem, M., Khan, K., Ma, J., … Han, H. (2024). Breathing in danger: Understanding the multifaceted impact of air pollution on health impacts. *Ecotoxicology and Environmental Safety, 280,* 116532.

Chen, Y., Song, L., Liu, Y., Yang, L., & Li, D. (2020). A review of the artificial neural network models for water quality prediction. *Applied Sciences, 10*(17), 5776.

Chisom, O., Biu, P., Umoh, A., Obaedo, B., Adegbite, A., & Abatan, A. (2024). Reviewing the role of AI in environmental monitoring and conservation: A data-driven revolution for our planet. *World Journal of Advanced Research and Reviews, 21*(1), 161–171.

Cipriano, C., Noce, S., Mereu, S., & Santini, M. (2025). Algorithms going wild–A review of machine learning techniques for terrestrial ecology. *Ecological Modelling, 506,* 111164.

Coţolan, L., & Moldovan, D. (2024). Applicability of pre-trained CNNs in temperate deforestation detection. *European Journal of Remote Sensing, 57*(1), 2367221.

Dalal, S. (2024). Optimizing convolutional neural network in predicting water quality of river water. *Frontiers in Health Informatics, 13*(4), 1548–1571.

Dang, W., Kim, S., Park, S., & Xu, W. (2024). The impact of economic and IoT technologies on air pollution: An AI-based simulation equation model using support vector machines. *Soft Computing-A Fusion of Foundations, Methodologies & Applications, 28*(4), 3591–3611. https://doi.org/10.1007/s00500-023-09622-7

Devender, B., Srinivas, C., Shivaprasad, K., Kumar, K., Nagavarapu, S., & Vimala, N. (2025). A machine learning-driven framework for real-time environmental pollution monitoring and prediction using IoT and remote sensing data. *International Journal of Environmental Sciences, 11*(10s), 714–723.

Dewi, D., Wei, A., Lin, L., & Heng, C. (2024). Water quality prediction using random forest algorithm and optimisation. *Journal of Applied Data Sciences, 5*(3), 1354–1362.

Dong, G., & Liu, H. (2018). *Feature engineering for machine learning and data analytics*. Boca Raton: CRC Press.

Dwivedi, Y., Sharma, A., Rana, N., Giannakis, M., Goel, P., & Dutot, V. (2023). Evolution of artificial intelligence research in technological forecasting and social change: Research topics, trends, and future directions. *Technological Forecasting and Social Change, 192*, 122579.

Elbaz, K., Shaban, W., Zhou, A., & Shen, S. (2023). Real time image-based air quality forecasts using a 3D-CNN approach with an attention mechanism. *Chemosphere, 333*, 138867.

Frank, J., Suesse, T., & Brenning, A. (2025). An assessment of spatial random forests for environmental mapping: The case of groundwater nitrate concentration. *Environmental Modelling & Software, 193*, 106626. https://doi.org/10.1016/j.envsoft.2025.106626

Greif, L., Röckel, F., Kimmig, A., & Ovtcharova, J. (2025). A systematic review of current AI techniques used in the context of the SDGs. *International Journal of Environmental Research, 19*(1), 1.

Guido, R., Ferrisi, S., Lofaro, D., & Conforti, D. (2024). An overview on the advancements of support vector machine models in healthcare applications: A review. *Information, 15*(4), 235.

Gupta, S., Singh, R., & Chaudhary, P. (2021). Advancing water quality assessment via artificial neural networks (ANNs). In K. A. Shukla (Ed.), *Spectroscopy and machine learning for water quality analysis* (pp. 5–1). Bristol, UK: IOP Publishing.

Habeeb, H., & Mustafa, Y. (2025). Analysing the impact of geoenvironmental factors on the spatiotemporal dynamics of forest cover via random forest. *Earth, 6*(1), 3.

Halevi, G., Moed, H., & Bar-Ilan, J. (2017). Suitability of google scholar as a source of scientific information and as a source of data for scientific evaluation—Review of the literature. *Journal of Informetrics, 11*(3), 823–834.

He, K., Liu, Y., Yuan, J., He, Z., Yin, Q., Xu, D., & Lu, H. (2024). Water quality ensemble prediction model for the urban water reservoir based on the hybrid long short-term memory (LSTM) network analysis. *AQUA—Water Infrastructure, Ecosystems and Society, 73*(8), 1621–1642.

Islam, F. (2025). The role of artificial intelligence in environmental monitoring for sustainable development and future perspectives. *Journal of Global Ecology and Environment, 21*(2), 164–179.

Jaffar, A., Thamrin, N., Ali, M., Misnan, M., & Yassin, A. (2022). Water quality prediction using LSTM-RNN: A review. *Journal of Sustainability Science and Management, 17*, 204–225.

Jain, A., Ong, S., Hautier, G., Chen, W., Richards, W., Dacek, S., … Persson, K. (2013). Commentary: The materials project: A materials genome approach to accelerating materials innovation. *APL Materials, 1*(1), 11002. https://doi.org/10.1063/1.4812323

Jerome Workman, J. (2025, April 22). *Smart sensors, cleaner earth using AI and IoT for pollution monitoring*. Retrieved from https://www.spectroscopyonline.com/view/smarter-sensors-cleaner-earth-using-ai-and-iot-for-pollution-monitoring

Junus, M., Nurcahyani, V., Saptono, R., Maulana, N., Putra, I., & Fahreza, Z. (2025). Implementation of random forest algorithm for air quality classification: A case study of DKI Jakarta's air quality index. *International Journal of Innovative Science and Research Technology, 10*(3), 2169–2173.

Khanam, R., Hussain, M., Hill, R., & Allen, P. (2024). A comprehensive review of convolutional neural networks for defect detection in industrial applications. *IEEE Access, 12*, 94250–94295. https://doi.org/10.1109/ACCESS.2024.3425166

Kumar, A., Shirin, S., Ansari, M., Pandey, G., Sharma, S., & Yadav, A. (2022). Fuzzy and neural network model-based environmental quality monitoring system: Past, present, and future. In *Modeling and simulation of environmental systems* (pp. 153–176). CRC Press.

Kumar, K., Palit, A., Sindhu, S., Divya, D., Yogita, E., Moharana, R., … Kumar, A. (2024). Artificial intelligence and machine learning in soil analysis innovations for sustainable agriculture: A review. *International Journal of Advanced Biochemistry, 8*(11), 869–878.

Lan, T., Hu, H., Jiang, C., Yang, G., & Zhao, Z. (2020). A comparative study of decision tree, random forest, and convolutional neural network for spread-F identification. *Advances in Space Research, 65*(8), 2052–2061.

Leong, W., Kelani, R., & Ahmad, Z. (2020). Prediction of air pollution index (API) using support vector machine (SVM). *Journal of Environmental Chemical Engineering, 8*(3), 103208.

Li, Y., Sha, Z., Tang, A., Goulding, K., & Liu, X. (2023). The application of machine learning to air pollution research: A bibliometric analysis. *Ecotoxicology and Environmental Safety, 257*, 114911.

Li, Z. (2025). Application of CNNs in feature learning for remote sensing data: A case study on land cover classification and environmental change detection. In *Proceedings of the 2nd International Conference on Data Analysis and Machine Learning* (pp. 354–358).

Locke, R., & Paschalidis, I. (2015). Detection and localisation of harmful atmospheric releases via support vector machines. *Environmental Systems Research, 4*(1), 2.

Mamat, N., Mohd Razali, S., & Hamzah, F. (2023). Enhancement of water quality index prediction using support vector machine with sensitivity analysis. *Frontiers in Environmental Science, 10*, 1061835.

Manisalidis, I., Stavropoulou, E., Stavropoulos, A., & Bezirtzoglou, E. (2020). Environmental and health impacts of air pollution: A review. *Frontiers in Public Health, 8*, 14.

Mezquita, B., Martín-Delgado, L., Wennberg-Capellades, L., & Borrego, Á. (2025). A comparison of OpenAlex with Scopus and Web of Science for tracking scholarly nursing literature. *SAGE Open Nursing, 11*, 23779608251361012.

Mienye, I., & Jere, N. (2024). A survey of decision trees: Concepts, algorithms, and applications. *IEEE Access, 12*, 86716–86727.

Mienye, I., Swart, T., & Obaido, G. (2024). Recurrent neural networks: A comprehensive review of architectures, variants, and applications. *Information, 15*(9), 517.

Mogollón-Sotelo, C., Casallas, A., Vidal, S., Celis, N., Ferro, C., & Belalcazar, L. (2021). A support vector machine model to forecast ground-level PM2.5 in a highly populated city with a complex terrain. *Air Quality, Atmosphere & Health, 14*(3), 399–409.

NIEHS. (2025, April 23). *Air pollution and your health*. Retrieved from https://www.nih.gov/health/topics/agents/air-pollution

Nisharga, M., & Narmadha, S. (2025). Predicting water quality parameters using LSTM models. *AIP Conference Proceedings, 3204*, 020010. AIP Publishing LLC.

Olawade, D., Wada, O., Ige, A., Egbewole, B., Olojo, A., & Oladapo, B. (2024). Artificial intelligence in environmental monitoring: Advancements, challenges, and future directions. *Hygiene and Environmental Health Advances, 12*, 100114. https://doi.org/10.1016/j.heha.2024.100114

Padhiary, M., Saha, D., Kumar, R., Sethi, L., & Kumar, A. (2024). Enhancing precision agriculture: A comprehensive review of machine learning and AI vision applications in all-terrain vehicle for farm automation. *Smart Agricultural Technology, 8*, 100483.

Palani, S., Liong, S., & Tkalich, P. (2008). An ANN application for water quality forecasting. *Marine Pollution Bulletin, 56*(9), 1586–1597.

Patel, P., Patel, S., Shah, K., Desai, K., Patel, S., Shah, M., & Patel, S. (2025). A systematic study on PM2.5 and PM10 concentration prediction in air pollution using machine learning and deep learning model. *Environmental Chemistry and Ecotoxicology, 7*, 1401–1415. https://doi.org/10.1016/j.enceco.2025.07.001

Popescu, S., Mansoor, S., Wani, O., Kumar, S., Sharma, V., Sharma, A., … Chung, Y. (2024). Artificial intelligence and IoT driven technologies for environmental pollution monitoring and management. *Frontiers in Environmental Science, 12*, 1336088.

Qi, C., Huang, S., & Wang, X. (2020). Monitoring water quality parameters of Taihu Lake based on remote sensing images and LSTM-RNN. *IEEE Access, 8*, 188068–188081.

Rawat, W., & Wang, Z. (2017). Deep convolutional neural networks for image classification: A comprehensive review. *Neural Computation, 29*(9), 2352–2449.

Riaz, M., Riaz, M., Rehman, A., Bindajam, A., Mallick, J., & Abdo, H. (2024). An integrated approach of support vector machine (SVM) and weight of evidence (WOE) techniques to map groundwater potential and assess water quality. *Scientific Reports, 4*(1), 26186.

Ruan, J., Cui, Y., Song, Y., & Mao, Y. (2023). A novel RF-CEEMD-LSTM model for predicting water pollution. *Scientific Reports, 13*(1), 20901.

Safder, U., Kim, J., Pak, G., Rhee, G., & You, K. (2022). Investigating machine learning applications for effective real-time water quality parameter monitoring in full-scale wastewater treatment plants. *Water, 14*(19), 3147.

Sarker, I. (2021). Machine learning: Algorithms, real-world applications and research directions. *SN Computer Science, 2*(3), 160.

Sedighkia, M., & Datta, B. (2023). Linking SVM based habitat model and evolutionary optimisation for managing environmental impacts of hydropower plants. *River Research and Applications, 39*(5), 897–910.

Singgalen, Y., Sutresno, S., Agus, M., & Dasra, R. (2025). Implementation of hybrid deep learning CNN model for multispectral satellite image classification in land change detection. *Journal of Theoretical and Applied Information Technology, 103*(6), 2579–2593.

Srivastava, A., & Sharma, H. (2024). AI-driven environmental monitoring using google earth engine. In B. pradhan & S. Mukhopadhyay (Eds.), *IoT Sensors* (Vol. 50, pp. 375–385) Cham, Switzerland: Springer Nature.

Sun, H., Fung, J., Chen, Y., Li, Z., Yuan, D., Chen, W., & Lu, X. (2022). Development of an LSTM broadcasting deep-learning framework for regional air pollution forecast improvement. *Geoscientific Model Development, 15*(22), 8439–8452.

Swapna, M., Sharma, Y., & Prasadh, B. (2020). CNN architectures: Alexnet, Lenet, VGG, Googlenet, Resnet. *International Journal of Recent Technology and Engineering, 8*(6), 953–960.

Sweileh, W. (2021). Bibliometric analysis of peer-reviewed literature on antimicrobial stewardship from 1990 to 2019. *Globalization and Health, 17*(1), 1.

TavallaieNejad, A., Vila, M., Paneiro, G., & Baptista, J. (2025). A systematic review of machine learning algorithms for soil pollutant detection using satellite imagery. *Remote Sensing, 17*(7), 1207.

Tsai, Y., Zeng, Y., & Chang, Y. (2018). Air pollution forecasting using RNN with LSTM. In *2018, IEEE 16th International Conference on Dependable, Autonomic and Secure Computing, 16th International Conference on Pervasive Intelligence and Computing, 4th International Conference on Big Data Intelligence and Computing and Cyber Science and Technology Congress* (pp. 1074–1079). IEEE.

Ukoba, K., Onisuru, O., Jen, T., Madyira, D., & Olatunji, K. (2025). Predictive modeling of climate change impacts using artificial intelligence: A review for equitable governance and sustainable outcome. *Environmental Science and Pollution Research,* 32, 10705–10724. https://doi.org/10.1007/s11356-025-36356-w

Utku, A., Can, U., Alpsülün, M., Balıkçı, H., Amoozegar, A., Pilatin, A., & Barut, A. (2025). Advancing air quality monitoring: Deep learning-based CNN-RNN hybrid model for PM2.5 forecasting. *Atmosphere, 16*(9), 1003.

Valadkhan, D., Moghaddasi, R., & Mohammadinejad, A. (2022). Groundwater quality prediction based on LSTM RNN: An Iranian experience. *International Journal of Environmental Science and Technology, 19*(11), 11397–11408.

Videnova, I., Nedialkov, D., Dimitrova, M., & Popova, S. (2006). Neural networks for air pollution nowcasting. *Applied Artificial Intelligence, 20*(6), 493–506.

Vij, P., & Prashant, P. (2024). Analyzing soil pollution by image processing and machine learning at contaminated agricultural field. *Natural and Engineering Sciences, 9*(2), 335–346.

Vinuesa, R., Azizpour, H., Leite, I., Balaam, M., Dignum, V., Domisch, S., … Fuso Nerini, F. (2020). The role of artificial intelligence in achieving the sustainable development goals. *Nature Communications, 11*(1), 233.

VVR, M., Silpa, N. K., Padmaja, S., Reddy, S., & GSLNVS, S. (2025). A resilient water quality investigation system using support vector machines and intelligent feature engineering. In *2025, 3rd International Conference on Sustainable Computing and Data Communication Systems (ICSCDS)* (pp. 1222–1228). IEEE.

Waqas, M., & Humphries, U. (2024). A critical review of RNN and LSTM variants in hydrological time series predictions. *MethodsX, 13*, 102946.

Wongburi, P., & Park, J. (2023). Prediction of wastewater treatment plant effluent water quality using recurrent neural network (RNN) models. *Water, 15*(19), 332.

Xayasouk, T., Lee, H., & Lee, G. (2020). Air pollution prediction using long short-term memory (LSTM) and deep autoencoder (DAE) models. *Sustainability, 12*(6), 2570.

Yuan, J., Dengxin, H., Yufeng, W., Xueting, Y., Huige, D., & Qing, Y. (2025). Attention mechanism based CNN-LSTM hybrid deep learning model for atmospheric ozone concentration prediction. *Scientific Reports, 15*(1), 21260.

Zavareh, M., Maggioni, V., & Zhang, X. (2023). Assessing the efficiency of a random forest regression model for estimating water quality indicators. *Meteorology Hydrology, and Water Management Research and Operational Applications, 11*(2), 52–69. https://doi.org/10.26491/mhwm/183734
Zhang, L. (2025). Air pollution. In *Sustainability Economics*. Cham: Springer. https://doi.org/10.1007/978-3-031-87829-9_10
Zhang, Q., Wang, R., Qi, Y., & Wen, F. (2022). A watershed water quality prediction model based on attention mechanism and Bi-LSTM. *Environmental Science and Pollution Research, 29*(50), 75664–75680.
Zhang, X., Shu, K., Rajkumar, S., & Sivakumar, V. (2021). Research on deep integration of application of artificial intelligence in environmental monitoring system and real economy. *Environmental Impact Assessment Review, 86*, 106499.
Zhao, T., Wang, S., Ouyang, C., Chen, M., Liu, C., Zhang, J., … Wang, F. (2024). Artificial intelligence for geoscience: Progress, challenges, and perspectives. *The Innovation, 5*(5), 100691. https://doi.org/10.1016/j.xinn.2024.100691

5

Machine Learning Predictive Modeling in Environmental Forecasting

Abstract

The use of emerging machine learning (ML) and artificial intelligence (AI)-based technologies in monitoring and management of the environment (MME) vis-à-vis environmental modelling and forecasting/prediction provides a comprehensive water quality (WA) and air quality (AQ) monitoring, precise disaster management and prediction (DMP), and the identification of pollutant sources. An overview of the advantageous aspects of MME, the drawbacks of traditional techniques, and possible AI-based solutions is given in this chapter. Highlighted are a number of noteworthy emerging ML- and AI-based technology applications in MME that demonstrate how they support efficient environmental forecasting or prediction. By making it possible to better comprehend, predict, and mitigate environmental dangers, emerging ML- and AI-based technologies improve MME. However, challenges like a lack of specialized ML- and AI-based professionals in the environmental field and issues with data access, control, and privacy stand in the way of achieving ML- and AI-based technologies' full potential. These challenges are especially noticeable in areas where technology infrastructure is still emerging. In order to safeguard sensitive data, the study promotes proactive data governance initiatives by governments. Notwithstanding these obstacles, emerging ML- and AI-based technologies in MME have a bright future ahead of them. Improvements in emerging ML- and AI-based algorithms, data-gathering methods, and processing capacity should increase the precision and effectiveness of pollution monitoring and control as well as forecasting or prediction.

5.1 Introduction

Environmental pollution (Aigbe et al., 2025; Eleryan et al., 2025; El-Nemr et al., 2025), especially pollution in the atmosphere, is the leading cause of mortality globally; it poses a serious threat to the health of humanity and is

DOI: 10.1201/9781003618584-5

one of the global issues (Hussain, Sipra, Waheed, & Ukhurebor, 2024; Olarte et al., 2025; Onyancha et al., 2021; Ukhurebor et al., 2024; 2022a). According to Kumari and Das (2023), numerous factors, such as automobile waste, excessive exhaust fumes, chemical effluents, toxic substances, and soil erosion, contribute to environmental pollution. Every individual, animal, and country is negatively impacted by environmental issues such as ozone layer depletion, acid rain, pollution in the atmosphere, urban sprawl, disposal of waste, aquatic pollution, climate (CM) change, and many more. Among the disastrous effects of the rise in environmental contaminants are heart disease, respiratory problems, cancer, and infertility (Figure 5.1). Since air/atmospheric pollution is a worldwide issue that impacts developing as well as developed nations, particularly those with huge cities, it may result in a number of detrimental effects on the environment, with acid rain, smog, biodiversity loss, CM change, and degradation of the ozone layer being the most notable (Alvarez-Tolentino & Suarez-Salas, 2020; Kerry et al., 2022; Olarte et al., 2025; Ukhurebor & Aidonojie, 2021; Ukhurebor et al., 2020; 2021a, 2021b; Ukhurebor, Singh, Nayak, & UK-Eghonghon, 2021c). Hence, the utilization of emerging machine learning (ML) and artificial intelligence (AI)-based technologies in monitoring and management of the environment

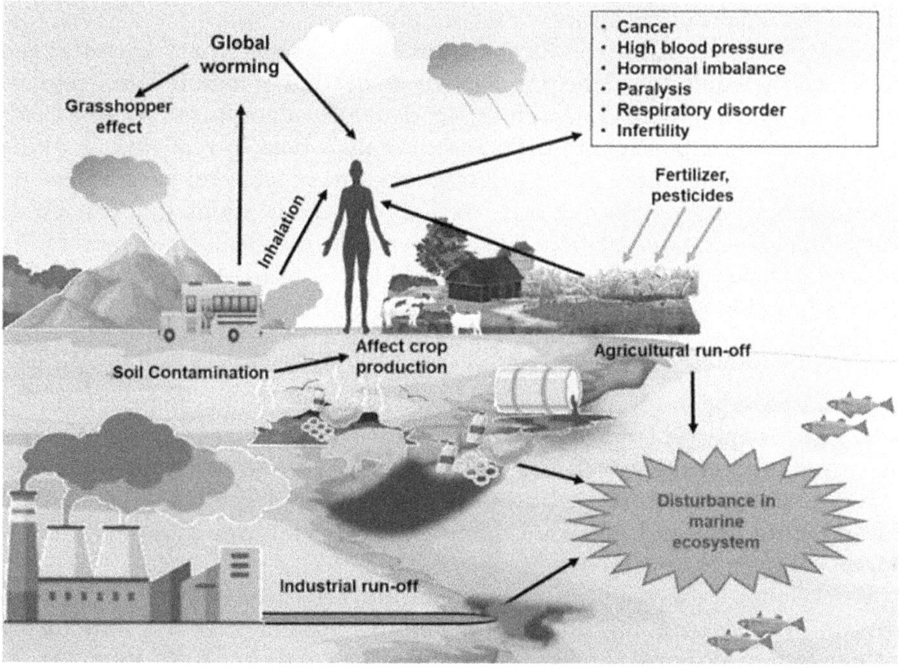

FIGURE 5.1
Causes and impacts of environmental pollution. (From Kumari and Das (2023), Springer Nature. With Permission.)

(MME) vis-à-vis environmental modelling and forecasting/prediction provides comprehensive water quality (WA) and air quality (AQ) monitoring, precise disaster management and prediction (DMP), and the identification of pollutant sources. These will assist in the provision and development of innovative approaches that will mitigate these detrimental effects on the environment.

There are now more options for MME and DMP owing to the combination of ML and AI with cutting-edge technologies like the "Internet of Things (IoT)" and "unmanned aerial vehicles (UAVs)", as well as "big data (BD)" platforms (Alotaibi & Nassif, 2024; Olarte et al., 2025). These multidisciplinary applications provide more thorough and real-time assessments of the environment by fusing the advantages of ML- and AI-based technologies with cutting-edge data collection and processing technology. In order to monitor AQ and identify harmful contaminants, Asha et al. (2022) designed an IoT-based "environmental toxicology for air/atmospheric pollution monitoring with AI techniques (ETAPM-AIT)" model, which integrates IoT-based sensors (SSs) with AI-based algorithms. Their method was developed to give agencies of government as well as industrial facilities real-time alerts, allowing for quicker reactions to incidents of air/atmospheric pollution. Their technique, which combines IoT and AI, is a major step forward in real-time MME and provides scalable solutions for businesses and towns trying to lessen the effects of air/atmospheric pollution.

Gonzalez et al. (2016) conducted another multidisciplinary investigation in which they monitored the populations of wildlife in remote forest regions using UAVs fitted with AI-based object detection algorithms. AI and UAVs together made it possible to collect and analyse data in real time, making it less difficult and more precise to track species ranges and keep an eye on the health of ecosystems. By offering real-time perceptions that can guide the management, preservation, and conservation as well as the sustainability of land policies, this system shows how AI-based technologies can improve conventional MME techniques.

The utilization of the "Google Earth Engine (GEE) platform" for BD processing in remote sensing (RS) applications was investigated by Tamiminia et al. (2020). The study processed large-scale satellite imaging datasets for CM assessment and land cover arrangement by utilizing emerging ML- and AI-based algorithms within the GEE platform. This research demonstrates the expanding use of BD platforms in MME, where large-scale deployment of emerging ML- and AI-based models enables real-time analysis of enormous volumes of geographical data.

Furthermore, the application of emerging ML- and AI-based technologies to MME is growing into new fields, including bioSSs and monitoring of healthcare systems (Aigbe, Ukhurebor, & Onyancha, 2023; Kerry et al., 2021; Paladhi et al., 2022; Singh, Ukhurebor, Singh, Adetunji, & Singh, 2022; Ukhurebor et al., 2022b). Zhang et al. (2025) showed how ML may be used to improve fluorescence-based detection techniques for environmental pollutants such as fluoride ions and aluminium. Their AI-enhanced bioSS demonstrated better sensitivity and accuracy than conventional detection techniques, underscoring emerging ML- and AI-based technologies' potential to increase safety for the public as well as MME of health systems.

Even though these multidisciplinary applications mark important developments in the field, issues still need to be resolved. Integrating emerging ML- and AI-based models with new machineries by a means which guarantees scalability and durability is one of the primary problems (Alotaibi & Nassif, 2024; Olarte et al., 2025). Huge volumes of high-quality data are necessary for many emerging ML- and AI-based systems, but these may not always be accessible, especially in areas with limited resources (Alotaibi & Nassif, 2024; Olarte et al., 2025). Future studies should concentrate on creating emerging ML- and AI-based models that are more resilient and flexible so they can operate well in low-resource settings. Further study is also required to address the ethical and legal issues surrounding the use of emerging ML- and AI-based technologies in MME systems vis-à-vis environmental modelling and forecasting/prediction, specifically those pertaining to data security, privacy, and algorithmic bias (Alotaibi & Nassif, 2024; Olarte et al., 2025).

5.2 Environmental Modelling and Forecasting/Prediction

Environmental modelling, which is one of the core aspects of MME, is essential for assessing and forecasting the intricate dynamics of our planet's ecosystems, from the management of natural resources to the optimization of agriculture and the comprehension of CM patterns (Aigbe & Ukhurebor, 2025; Alotaibi & Nassif, 2024; Olarte et al., 2025; Ukhurebor & Aigbe, 2024; Ukhurebor, Aigbe, & Onyancha, 2023; Ukhurebor et al., 2021a, 2021b, 2021c; Wang & Wu, 2024). These modelling attempts have historically mostly depended on statistical and physical process-based methods that are based on basic principles and empirical facts. These approaches, however, frequently call for substantial contributions of domain-specific information from experts in the field, which can slow down the rate of discovery and make it more difficult to completely capture complex environmental events. Environmental modelling now has revolutionary possibilities thanks to the quick development of computational power and ML techniques. Robust ML- and AI-based algorithms, such as deep NNs, have shown an amazing capacity for generalization and approximation from data, learning to represent extremely complex systems with less need for domain experts' prior knowledge (Alotaibi & Nassif, 2024; Wang & Wu, 2024). Innovative ML- and AI-based technologies such as recurrent NNs and CNNs have shown exceptional proficiency in modelling time series (TSs) data and image data, respectively, two essential data modalities in environmental research. Although innovative ML- and AI-based technologies provide strong tools, their full potential must be realized by properly articulating environmental challenges in mathematical terms and modifying these broad approaches to achieve the best results on tasks particular to a given domain (Wang & Wu, 2024). Research is still being done to close this gap between state-of-the-art ML- and AI-based capabilities and the particular difficulties of environmental modelling. To drive the limits of what could possibly be modelled as well as predicted, innovative ML- and AI-based technology frameworks customized for environmental data are required (Alotaibi & Nassif, 2024; Olarte et al., 2025; Wang & Wu, 2024).

By presenting innovative techniques and a range of applications, this chapter, as well as this book, seeks to contribute to this developing hybridization of environmental modelling as well as innovative ML- and AI-based technologies. In this chapter, several reported studies as well as publications have been strategically selected to demonstrate how innovative ML- and AI-based technologies may advance environmental modelling across a variety of disciplines following a thorough peer-review process. These reviewed publications concentrate on developing appropriate innovative ML- and AI-based technologies to address various environmental science objectives, including general prediction, modelling, and optimization from real-world data.

5.2.1 Innovative Predictive Modelling in Environmental Forecasting/Prediction

Reportedly, the application and integration of predictive modelling (Akhetuamen, Konyeha, & Ukhurebor, 2025), such as innovative ML- and AI-based technologies are used in several types of studies to track environmental variables and forecast future circumstances in areas such as greenhouse (GH) gas concentrations, wildfires, urban AQ, as well as the modifications in lake surface area (Olarte et al., 2025; Wang & Wu, 2024).

Li, He, Xue, Liu, and Gao. (2024b) presented a hybrid model for predicting GH TSs in their study. Their study proposes an innovative predicting model, "Single Dendrite Neurone (SDN)", that utilizes the "seasonal-trend decomposition" as a preprocessing technique and the SDN as a nonlinear fitter to tackle GH TSs predictions. In GH farming, SSs are frequently used to monitor constantly changing CM conditions and produce time-related data. The prediction of these TSs contributes in no little way to GH cultivation. Several studies focus on the chaotic aspects of the TSs and develop several ML-based models but ignore their inherent features, such as seasonality as well as tendency. While the well-developed neurone structure affords SDN time efficiency, the deconstruction gives SDN freedom to handle each component independently. Consequently, the results from the experiments demonstrate that the suggested SDN not only outperforms the popular ML-based models but also demonstrates robustness when taking into account customized variables and dataset outliers, increasing the likelihood that SDN will be used in real-world utilization scenarios.

Luo, Wang, and Gates (2024) used multivariate "long short-term memory (LSTM)"; their study attempts to examine how climatic variables such as temperature, wind direction, and wind speed affect the predictions of methane concentration TSs data. According to the results from their study, including climatic variables improves the LSTM model's prediction power. Though temperature seems to have a greater effect on increasing predictive accuracy than wind speed and direction, the data indicate that it is uncertain which variable has the greatest influence on the improvements. The findings also imply that performance forecasting is unaffected by input data variance.

Jiao, Choi, Wang, and Farahi (2024) used innovative ML- and AI-based technologies to evaluate AQ status in Chicago by combining SS data and street view photos. The status of the AQ in Chicago was investigated using "Google Street View (GSV)" images and "Microsoft's Project Eclipse" urban CM SSs, which combine traditional land use data with GSV photographic evidence. The study uses ML techniques like "XGBoost regression and SHapley Additive exPlanations (SHAP)" to analyse the data in order to determine how land use affects AQ. The purpose of principal component analysis (PCA) was to comprehend spatial relationships. Key findings showed that, with the exception of the "Northern Intersection of West Belmont Avenue", where serious AQ concerns were found, the majority of SS locations had AQ that was in line with the city's predetermined criteria. Identification of the impacts of land use on the quality of the air was improved by the use of GSV imagery, which offered a comprehensive, multi-angle perspective of metropolitan areas. According to the study, the effects of various land use types on AQ vary; particularly near the "Intersection of West Belmont Avenue", transportation as well as land use factors significantly worsen the contamination of the air/atmosphere. Based on these results from the study, in order to reduce possible dangers to AQ, local governments should address particular land use and built environment characteristics in particular locations, such as West Belmont Avenue. The results also demonstrate how incorporating street view photography into traditional land use techniques can enhance AQ evaluation and urban planning initiatives. The integration of more sophisticated imagery and the usage of urban temperature SSs may prove advantageous for future studies.

Khalaf, Jouibary, and Jahdi (2024) explored the "performance analysis of ConvLSTM, FlamMap, and CA algorithms to predict wildfire spread in Golestan National Park, NE Iran" using DL, simulation, and cellular automata techniques. In the "Golestan National Park (GNP)", a region of the Hyrcanian forest and one of the most fire-prone locations, the effectiveness of three well-known algorithms for predicting the spread of wildfires, "Cellular Automata (CA), FlamMap, and Convolutional LSTM (ConvLSTM) network", was assessed in this study. The Scott and Burgan model list for each method was used to choose the fuel models in the study area. When determining the fuel type and density levels, the CA algorithm also took the vegetation stand features into account. About 325 fire simulations were carried out using the FlamMap and BehavePlus fire modelling tools to generate the training data for the ConvLSTM. According to the results, the ConvLSTM algorithm performed better than the other two algorithms in terms of the Sorensen coefficient, Kappa, and total accuracy. For each of the fires, the ConvLSTM algorithm produced the highest Sorensen coefficient values, which ranged between 0.78 and 0.82; in contrast, FlamMap and CA exhibited rates of underestimation and overestimation, respectively. The CA algorithm outperformed the other algorithms in terms of the rate of spread. In order to enhance wildfire management and mitigation initiatives in fire-prone regions, this study offers insights into how well various algorithms forecast burnt regions and the extent of wildfire expansion.

Also, He, Li, Qian, and Hu (2024a) employed TSs clustering (CT) to investigate the dynamics of lake areas. Due to its unique geographical setting and sizable lake groups, the Qinghai-Tibet Plateau is a crucial area of study for regional interactions with CM change and global warming, as reported in this their study. Its 149 representative lakes serve as the research subject, and the variation of the lake dimensions, the temporal division of changes in the CM, and the influence of CM factors on the lake area rate of growth are all investigated employing pertinent lake region data between 1985 and 2020. The following are the primary techniques and outcomes:

a. Three patterns of region change, "C1, C2, and C3 modes", which exhibit a sluggish development trend, a robust fluctuating pattern, as well as a considerable growth trend, respectively, are summarized by mining the form similarity of lake change in area in the utilizing the TSs CT algorithm.
b. The CM area segmentation locations for lakes are most prevalent from 1995 to 2005. This was done by combining the CT findings of the lake regional CM with the ideal segmentation location index of the binary sequence to determine the date of the optimal segmentation location for all lakes.
c. Precipitation has the largest impact on the lake region, followed by surface temperature, when lakes in C3 mode are studied employing the "XGBoost model" as the regression model for obtaining the feature relevance determining lake development rate. Precipitation has the greatest impact, followed by evaporation, when a double ML model was developed to perform causal analysis and produce an objective prediction of the lake region growth rate influenced by CM features. The techniques employed and the outcomes offer a fresh viewpoint on how to comprehend the changing CM as well as lake response.

Even though a lot of research has been carried out on forecasting carbon emissions, such as that of He et al. (2024b), where they presented three fluctuation density (FD3) which was a novel DL framework for predicting carbon emissions, as well as other reported studies carbon emission forecasting such as Wang, Li, and Khan (2022), Cui et al. (2023), Nibbering and Paap (2024), and Wu, Chen, Li, and Shi (2024), there are still few high-accuracy models that are appropriate for small-sample scenarios that can be used to predict short-range emission patterns in high-carbon regions such as "Shandong" in the study of Wu, Gong, Zhang, and Liu (2025). A fractional-order (FO) accumulative grey model (GM) was used in this work to forecast and analyse Shandong's emissions of carbon. The results provided more scientific backing for the development of distinct carbon peaking routes and the enhancement of the province's energy and industrial frameworks. This study has the potential for innovation in two ways: firstly, an enhanced FO GM prediction framework is first shown. Through the use of particle swarm optimization techniques and FO calculus, the model successfully lowers prediction errors in the face of sparse observational data, leading to increased accuracy. Secondly, the chosen model works especially well for small-sample evaluation and is well-suited for predicting short-range trends or datasets with no discernible saturation patterns. An essential methodological addition to current research is the use of the FO cumulative GM for short-range emissions of carbon analysis at the province level. As a result of these predictions, this study suggests that "Shandong" should improve policies and market coordination processes in order to reinforce institutional benefits and challenges, encourage green transformation (sustainable development) and industry upgrading in order to foster innovative drivers of economic growth, and expedite the optimization of its supply of energy structure to develop a clean as well as a low-carbon energy system. In addition to offering methodological references for other industrialized provinces dealing with comparable issues, these findings give Shandong a solid foundation for achieving its emissions peak and ecological neutrality targets.

5.2.2 Innovative Predictive Modelling in Agriculture, Land Use, and the Management of Natural Resources

Several reported studies also apply innovation in predictive modelling to agriculture, land use, and management of natural resources concerns (Alotaibi & Nassif, 2024; Kerry et al., 2022; Ndunagu, Ukhurebor, Akaaza, & Onyancha, 2022; Olarte et al., 2025; Wang & Wu, 2024). In order to satisfy people's nutritional needs in the modern world, food security is an essential necessity. By 2050, the demand for food will have grown by 70–100% due to population growth. Thus, there is a pressing need to create a method that would help farmers forecast crop production precisely and promptly before harvest. In order to extract the nonlinear complicated interactions among crop traits, Saini and Nagpal (2024), in their study, suggested an optimized hybrid CNN with bidirectional LSTM that was inspired by nature. Using a particle swarm optimization technique, this hybrid DL model was optimized to automatically choose the best hyperparameters for predicting wheat yield. Using both the spatial and temporal features of wheat crops, the suggested model was designed for estimating wheat output in significant wheat-producing regions in India between 2000 and 2018. The study was carried out by combining soil factors from the October to April season, historical yield, weather data, and indices produced from RS. Additionally, we used publicly accessible datasets, including Agro_data, Soybean_data, and FAO data, to assess the performance of the suggested model with respect to the "mean absolute error (MAE), root mean square error (RMSE), and mean squared error (MSE)". According to the research findings, the suggested PSO-CNN-Bi-LSTM approach surpassed the current "CNN, LSTM, CNN-LSTM, CNN-Bi-LSTM, CNN-LSTM-PSO, CNN-Bi-LSTM-BO-GO, and NN methods", achieving 0.39, 0.18 and 0.42 for MAE, MSE, and RMSE (tonnes/ha), respectively. Their results showed that the suggested approach might be a viable substitute for crop yield prediction.

Changes in land cover may possess an impact on the amounts of soil organic carbon (SOC) in top-soils and subsoils. Li, Liang, Awada, Hiller, and Kaiser (2024a), in their study, suggest using cutting-edge ML technologies to forecast the amounts of SOC in the soil's composition profile (0–300 cm). In particular, they evaluated the application of the recently created light gradient boosting machine (GBM) and contrasted its precision for the prediction of SOC with seven widely used algorithms: multiple linear regression, random forest (RF), multilayer perceptrons, GBM, extreme GBM, support vector machine, LASSO, and RF. Samples of soil were taken at six different soil levels (0–10, 10–30, 30–100, 100–170, 170–240, and 240–300 cm) under three different vegetation covers: ponderosa pine (*Pinus ponderosa*), eastern redcedar (*Juniperus virginiana*), and native open C4 grass community. They measured the cation exchange capacity, pH, Na, electrical conductivity, plant-available nutrients, soil density of the bulk, and SOC concentration. To model SOC, we employed these soil characteristics as predictors. Ponderosa pine and eastern redcedar forests showed increases in the measured SOC in topsoil but decreases in subsurface as compared to the native grasslands. These variations were faithfully replicated by the ML models. The gradient boosted tree-based models, or GBM and LGBM, performed the best (R^2 = 0.920 and 0.918, respectively). The measured mean SOC was 2.360 g kg^{-1}, while the GBM and long GBM predicted SOC, averaged over all vegetation and soil depths, were 2.362 and 2.343 g kg^{-1}. The adverse consequences of changing land cover on subsurface SOC concentrations have been demonstrated by this study. Additionally, they verified the accuracy of a recently developed ML algorithm, specifically long GBM, in SOC modelling as well as its reactivity to changes in land cover and soil depth. Our findings aid in the development of integrated MME plans and an improved understanding of SOC dynamics.

A complex process, tree decline is a natural result of numerous anthropogenic, physiological, and climatic influences. Finding the location and severity of declining processes and what underlies their dynamics across different ecological environments is the main task of monitoring them. For this, satellite and aerial RS techniques provide an affordable and spatially explicit substitute for field methods. Due to their limitations in the spectral and spatial domains, consumer-grade unmanned aerial vehicles (UAVs) are seldom suitable for use as stand-alone tools for large-area monitoring. They may, however, be successfully combined with satellite data to release their information for later landscape-level upscaling. By connecting UAV-RGB data with "space-borne multispectral and digital elevation model (DEM) data" over 15 Persian oak-dominated forest locations spanning the latitudinal gradient of the Zagros Forests in western Iran. Hence, Ghasemi, Latifi, and Pourhashemi (2024) developed an innovative two-step method to characterize the severity of tree loss. In the semi-arid Zagros mountains of Iran, this study explores how to (a) use UAVs as reference data across several structurally distinct Persian oak-dominated sites; (b) connect "UAV, Copernicus DEM, and Sentinel-2 data" to retrieve decline information in a model-driven context; and (c) use a global variance-based sensitivity evaluation to assess the sensitiveness of models. The findings indicated a strong correlation between UAV and field data on decline intensity, allowing for the estimation of decline severity utilizing space-borne data utilizing semi-parametric "generalised additive model (GAM)" and non-parametric RF techniques using sampled UAV data as a reference. In conclusion, this study established a baseline for multi-scale tree decline assessment utilizing partially free and budgeted data sources, which can be very beneficial from a scientific and technological as well as a practical standpoint for monitoring and management in hilly, isolated, sparse, and continually deteriorating forest regions.

China's economy has benefited greatly from tourism, which also uses a lot of energy and contributes to environmental degradation. Hence, Zhao Wu, Wang, Sun, and Wang (2024), in their study, examine techniques for reducing consumption of energy in tourism and examine the factors influencing energy consumption in seven Chinese provinces using the "logarithmic mean Divisia index (LMDI)" approach and K-means CT. More specifically, this study disintegrates the factors that affect tourism consumption of energy in each region into six categories and determines the factors that influence how much energy is consumed. Also, using the most recent dynamic impacting elements as CT factors, the K-means CT approach was employed to classify different regions into three different categories. Based on the features of each group, specific recommendations are provided for each province. In order to identify targeted energy optimization solutions for the energy consumption of the Chinese tourism industry, this study integrates CT analysis with the LMDI model.

According to Kumar, Sharda, Goyal, Siag, and Kaur (2024), for water resources to be monitored and managed effectively, reference evapotranspiration (ET) estimation must be accurate. However, because of its complex and nonlinear impact on several CM-related variables, predicting the ET is challenging. They used "artificial neural networks (ANNs)" to reproduce ET at three distinct stations in the Punjabi Malwa region: "Ludhiana, Bathinda, and Faridkot". Several combinations of meteorological features, referred to as (S1–S7) scenarios, were used to compare the model to the traditional FAO-56 Penman–Monteith (PM) approach. The model was assessed using statistical measures such as r, R^2, MSE, RMSE, NRMSE, and NSE. With RMSE (0.154, 0.246, and 0.298) and NSE (0.9933, 0.9849, and 0.9709) values, the results indicate that S1, with the greatest number of variables, did exceptionally well. With RMSE (0.218, 0.316, and 0.307) and NSE (0.9877, 0.9751, and 0.9699) for the stations in "Ludhiana, Bathinda, and Faridkot", respectively, S2 (Tmax, Tmin, n, u2) came in second. Scenario S6, which solely used relative humidity and air/atmosphere temperature, performed the worst of all the situations. Additionally, the produced ANN models demonstrated their superiority by outperforming conventional empirical models, even when the input variables were equal. The ANN models at the Ludhiana station performed better than the others in almost every scenario because of the trustworthy dataset. Because there were more missing values in the inconsistent dataset, the ANN models did not perform well for the "Bathinda and Faridkot stations". The developed ANN-based model is anticipated to allow effective crop planning and irrigation, as well as monitoring and management of water resources, especially in areas with not enough data availability.

5.2.3 Innovative Predictive Modelling in Environmental Pollution and Uncertainty

When developing remediation techniques for decommissioned industrial locations, it is crucial to estimate the volume of soil that exceeds a certain contamination threshold (Alotaibi & Nassif, 2024; Olarte et al., 2025; Wang & Wu, 2024). In actuality, interpolation techniques and preliminary sampling surveys serve as the main foundation for the volume estimate. However, there may be concerns to the economy and environment if the volume is not accurately anticipated. Techniques with a geostatistical focus have been developed to use uncertainty ranges to more accurately evaluate the volume. Hence, Guridi, Chassagne, Pryet, and Atteia (2024) used DL to quantify and characterize environmental pollution in their study. In this paper, they suggest a methodology called "Evol" that combines DL and traditional non-parametrical interpolation approaches in order to improve volume estimation and lower uncertainty ranges. In "Evol", a synthetic model was developed from an actual polluted site, descriptive characteristics (features) are extracted from several sample sets, and the volume calculation error is assessed. The features are then used to train a deep NN model, which may be used to predict the volume and range of uncertainty for every given sample. This methodology's low RMSE of 0.008 across the majority of sample sets indicated adequate precision in error prediction. Furthermore, this method reduced the interval size by up to 89%, producing probability volume intervals that were lower than those produced by traditional methods.

More research that will stimulate and integrate innovative ML- and AI-based technologies and environmental science by sharing cutting-edge findings that utilize innovative ML- and AI-based technologies to assess contaminants, optimize resource use, and monitor environmental health is still required (Alotaibi & Nassif, 2024; Olarte et al., 2025; Wang & Wu, 2024). The complex natural processes that support our planet can be more accurately, scalable, and data-driven modelled as a result of such interdisciplinary initiatives are all welcome innovations (Alotaibi & Nassif, 2024; Olarte et al., 2025; Wang & Wu, 2024).

5.3 Conclusion

Considerable advances have been made in the development of models and methodological advancements for the forecasting of innovative predictive modelling (emerging ML- and AI-based technologies) in environmental modelling and forecasting/prediction, especially in carbon emissions. GM prediction models have attracted a lot of interest among current methods because of their excellent performance when dealing with small-sample datasets and scenarios with little information. In conclusion, this chapter suggests an enhanced FO GM forecasting model using emerging ML- and AI-based technologies in contrast to previous research that relied on traditional GMs. This suggested method will successfully lower prediction errors frequently connected with conventional GMs in data-sparse scenarios by combining FO calculus with a particle swarm optimization algorithm. Additionally, more research should be done that will use a GM designed especially for little-sample data analysis, as opposed to methods that use FO logistic GMs for the predictions of carbon emission. A model that shows enhanced effectiveness in short-range forecasting and when analysing data that does not display saturation patterns needs to be proposed, even though FO logistic models are better suited for medium- and long-term predictions/forecasts.

References

Aigbe, U. O., & Ukhurebor, K. E. (2025). *Applications of magnetic nanomaterials for environmental sustainability under the influence of magnetic field.* United Kingdom: Institute of Physics (IOP) Publishing. https://doi.org/10.1088/978-0-7503-6377-8

Aigbe, U. O., Ukhurebor, K. E., & Onyancha, R. B. (Eds.) (2023). *Synthesis, characterization and applications of magnetic nanomaterials: Recent advances.* Switzerland: Springer Nature. https://doi.org/10.1007/978-3-031-36088-6

Aigbe, U. O., Ukhurebor, K. E., Onyancha, R. B., Osibote, A. O., Hassaan, M. A., El-Katory, M. R., & El Nemr, A. (2025). Prediction of methylene blue dye sorption to sulfonated Date palm kernel biochar using statistical regression and machine learning methods and DFT studies. *Journal of Molecular Liquids, 429*, 127547.

Akhetuamen, S. O., Konyeha, S., & Ukhurebor, K. E. (2025). Integrating predictive modeling with sentiment analysis for Lassa fever prediction. *Next Research, 2*(3), 100586.

Alotaibi, E., & Nassif, N. (2024). Artificial intelligence in environmental monitoring: In-depth analysis. *Discover Artificial Intelligence, 4*(84). https://doi.org/10.1007/s44163-024-00198-1

Alvarez-Tolentino, D., & Suarez-Salas, L. (2020). Apportionment of emission sources of PM10 and PM2.5 at urban sites of Valley, Peru. *Revista Internacional de Contaminación Ambiental, 36*, 875–892.

Asha, P., Natrayan, L., Geetha, B. T., Beulah, J. R., Sumathy, R., Varalakshmi, G., & Neelakandan, S. (2022). IoT enabled environmental toxicology for air pollution monitoring using AI techniques. *Environmental Research.* https://doi.org/10.1016/j.envres.2021.112574

Cui, T., Shi, Y., Lv, B., Ding, R., & Li, X. (2023). Federated learning with SARIMA-based clustering for carbon emission prediction. *Journal of Cleaner Production, 420*, 139069.

Eleryan, A., Aigbe, U. O., Ukhurebor, K. E., Hassaan, M. A., Ragab, S., Osibote, A. O., Hossain, I., & El Nemr, A. (2025). Adsorption of acid yellow 36 and direct blue 86 dyes to Delonix Regia Biochar-Sulphur. *Scientific Reports, 15*, 3448.

El-Nemr, M. A., Aigbe, U. O., Ukhurebor, K. E., Obodo, K., Awe, A. A., Hassaan, M. A., … El Nemr, A. (2025). Modelling of a new form of nitrogen doped activated carbon for adsorption of various dyes and hexavalent chromium ions. *Scientific Reports, 15*, 3896.

Ghasemi, M., Latifi, H., & Pourhashemi, M. (2024). Integrating UAV and freely available space-borne data to describe tree decline across semi-arid mountainous forests. *Environmental Modeling & Assessment, 29*, 549–568. https://doi.org/10.1007/s10666-023-09911-3

Gonzalez, L. F., Montes, G. A., Puig, E., Johnson, S., Mengersen, K., & Gaston, K. J. (2016). Unmanned aerial vehicles (UAVs) and artificial intelligence revolutionizing wildlife monitoring and conservation. *Sensors (Switzerland).* https://doi.org/10.3390/s16010097

Guridi, I., Chassagne, R., Pryet, A., & Atteia, O. (2024). Uncertainty quantification of contaminated soil volume with deep neural networks and predictive models. *Environmental Modeling & Assessment, 29*, 621–640. https://doi.org/10.1007/s10666-023-09924-y

He, H., Li, W., & Qian, M., & Hu, S. (2024a). Time series clustering and influencing factors analysis on Qinghai-Tibet plateau Lake area change. *Environmental Modeling & Assessment, 29*, 503–516. https://doi.org/10.1007/s10666-023-09913-1

He, H., Liu, T., Li, Q., Yang, J., Wang, R. L., & Gao, S. (2024b). A novel FD3 framework for carbon emissions prediction. *Environmental Modeling and Assessment, 29*(3), 455–469. https://doi.org/10.1007/s10666-023-09918-w

Hussain, A., Sipra, H. F. K., Waheed, A., & Ukhurebor, K. E. (2024). Exploring the academic perceptions of climate engineering in developing countries. *Atmósfera, 38*, 311–325.

Jiao, J., Choi, S. J., Wang, H., & Farahi, A. (2024). Evaluating air quality status in Chicago: Application of Street view imagery and urban climate sensors. *Environmental Modeling & Assessment, 29*, 471–488. https://doi.org/10.1007/s10666-023-09894-1

Kerry, R. G., Montalbo, F. J. P., Das, R., Patra, S., Mahapatra, G. P., Maurya, G. K., … Rou, J. R. (2022). An overview of remote monitoring methods in biodiversity conservation. *Environmental Science and Pollution Research, 2022*, 1–43.

Kerry, R. G., Ukhurebor, K. E., Kumari, S., Maurya, G. K., Patra, S., Panigrahi, B., … Patra, J. K. (2021). A comprehensive review on the applications of nano-biosensor based approaches for non-communicable and communicable disease detection. *Biomaterials Science, 9*, 3576–3602.

Khalaf, M., Jouibary, A., & Jahdi, S. S. (2024). Performance analysis of ConvLSTM, FlamMap, and CA algorithms to predict wildfire spread in Golestan National Park, NE Iran. *Environmental Modeling & Assessment, 29*, 489–502. https://doi.org/10.1007/s10666-024-09956-y

Kumar, S., Sharda, R., Goyal, P., Siag, M., & Kaur, P. (2024). Reference evapotranspiration modelling using artificial neural networks under scenarios of limited weather data: A case study in the Malwa region of Punjab. *Environmental Modeling & Assessment, 29*, 589–620. https://doi.org/10.1007/s10666-023-09930-0

Kumari, S., & Das, S. (2023). Bacterial enzymatic degradation of recalcitrant organic pollutants: Catabolic pathways and genetic regulations. *Environmental Science and Pollution Research, 30*, 79676–79705. https://doi.org/10.1007/s11356-023-28130-7

Li, L., Liang, W., Awada, T., Hiller, J., & Kaiser, M. (2024a). Machine learning for modeling soil organic carbon as affected by land cover change in the Nebraska Sandhills, USA. *Environmental Modeling & Assessment, 29*, 535–547. https://doi.org/10.1007/s10666-024-09973-x

Li, Q., He, H., Xue, C., Liu, T., & Gao, S. (2024b). A seasonal-trend decomposition and single dendrite neuron-based predicting model for greenhouse time series. *Environmental Modeling & Assessment, 29*, 427–440. https://doi.org/10.1007/s10666-023-09931-z

Luo, R., Wang, J., & Gates, I. (2024). Forecasting methane data using multivariate long short-term memory neural networks. *Environmental Modeling & Assessment, 29*, 441–454. https://doi.org/10.1007/s10666-024-09957-x

Ndunagu, J. N., Ukhurebor, K. E., Akaaza, M. D., & Onyancha, R. B. (2022). Development of a wireless sensor network and IoT-based smart irrigation system. *Applied and Environmental Soil Science, 7678570*, 1–13.

Nibbering, D., & Paap, R. (2024). Forecasting carbon emissions using asymmetric grouping. *Journal of Forecasting, 43*, 2228–2256.

Olarte, E., Gutierrez, J., Roque, G., Soria, J. J., Fernandez, H., Carpio, J. E. P., & Poma, O. (2025). Predictive model with machine learning for environmental variables and PM2.5 in Huachac, Junín, Perú. *Atmosphere, 16*(3), 323. https://doi.org/10.3390/atmos16030323

Onyancha, R. B., Ukhurebor, K. E., Aigbe, U. O., Osibote, O. A., Kusuma, H. S., Darmokoesoemo, H., & Balogun, V. A. (2021). A systematic review on the detection and monitoring of toxic gases using carbon nanotube-based biosensors. *Sensing and Bio-Sensing Research, 34*, 100463.

Paladhi, A. G., Manohar, M. V., Pal, K., Vallinayagam, S., Packirisamy, A. S. B., Bashreer, V. A., … Ukhurebor, K. E. (2022). Novel electrochemical biosensor key significance of smart intelligence (IoMT & IoHT) of COVID-19 virus control management. *Process Biochemistry, 122*, 105–109.

Saini, P., & Nagpal, B. (2024). PSO-CNN-Bi-LSTM: A hybrid optimization-enabled deep learning model for smart farming. *Environmental Modeling & Assessment, 29*, 517–534. https://doi.org/10.1007/s10666-023-09920-2

Singh, R. P., Ukhurebor, K. E., Singh, J., Adetunji, C. O., & Singh, K. R. B. (Eds.) (2022). *Nanobiosensors for environmental monitoring - Fundamentals and application.* Switzerland: Springer Nature. https://doi.org/10.1007/978-3-031-16106-3

Tamiminia, H., Salehi, B., Mahdianpari, M., Quackenbush, L., Adeli, S., & Brisco, B. (2020). Google earth engine for geo-big data applications: A meta-analysis and systematic review. *ISPRS Journal of Photogrammetry and Remote Sensing, 164*, 152–70. https://doi.org/10.1016/j.isprsjprs.2020.04.001

Ukhurebor, K. E., & Aidonojie, P. A. (2021). The influence of climate change on food innovation technology: Review on topical developments and legal framework. *Agriculture & Food Security, 10*(50), 1–14.

Ukhurebor, K. E., & Aigbe, U. O. (Eds.) (2024). *Environmental applications of magnetic sorbents.* United Kingdom: Institute of Physics (IOP) Publishing. https://doi.org/10.1088/978-0-7503-5909-2

Ukhurebor, K. E., Aigbe, U. O., Onyancha, R. B., Nwankwo, W., Osibote, O. A., Paumo, H. K., … Siloko, I. U. (2021a). Effect of hexavalent chromium on the environment and removal techniques: A review. *Journal of Environmental Management, 280*, 111809.

Ukhurebor, K. E., Aigbe, U. O., Onyancha, R. B., UK-Eghonghon, G., Balogun, V. A., Egielewa, P. E., … Darmokoesoemo, H. (2022a). Greenhouse gases emission: Perception during the COVID-19 pandemic. *BioMed Research International, 6166276*(1), 12.

Ukhurebor, K. E., Aigbe, U. O., & Onyancha, R. B. (Eds.) (2023). *Adsorption applications for environmental sustainability.* United Kingdom: Institute of Physics (IOP) Publishing. https://doi.org/10.1088/978-0-7503-5598-8

Ukhurebor, K. E., Aigbe, U. O., Onyancha, R. B., Athar, H., Okundaye, B., Aidonojie, P. A., … Darmokoesoemo, H. (2024). Environmental influence of gas flaring: Perspective from the Niger Delta region of Nigeria. *Geofluids, 1321022*, 1–17.

Ukhurebor, K. E., Azi, S. O., Aigbe, U. O., Onyancha, R. B., & Emegha, J. O. (2020). Analysing the uncertainties between reanalysis meteorological data and ground measured meteorological data. *Measurement, 165*, 108110.

Ukhurebor, K. E., Hussain, A., Adetunji, C. O., Aigbe, U. O., Onyancha, R. B., & Abifarin, O. (2021b). Environmental implications of petroleum spillages in the Niger Delta region of Nigeria: A review. *Journal of Environmental Management, 293*, 112872.

Ukhurebor, K. E., Onyancha, R. B., Aigbe, U. O., UK-Eghonghon, G., Kerry, R. G., Kusuma, H. S., … Balogun, V. A. (2022b). A methodical review on the applications and potentialities of using nanobiosensors for diseases diagnosis. *BioMed Research International, 1682502*, 1–20.

Ukhurebor, K. E., Singh, K. R. B., Nayak, V., & UK-Eghonghon, G. (2021c). Influence of SARS-CoV-2 pandemic: A review from the climate change perspective. *Environmental Science: Processes & Impacts, 23*, 1060–1078.

Wang, H., Li, B., & Khan, M. Q. (2022). Prediction of Shanghai electric power carbon emissions based on improved STIRPAT model. *Sustainability, 14*, 13068.

Wang, Y.-G., & Wu, J. (2024). Foreword: Machine learning in environmental modelling. *Environmental Modeling & Assessment, 29,* 425–426. https://doi.org/10.1007/s10666-024-09981-x

Wu, L., Gong, W.-F., Zhang, W.-J., & Liu, X.-Y. (2025). Fractional-order accumulative gray model for carbon emission prediction: A case study of Shandong province. *Fractal and Fractional, 9*(9), 595.

Wu, Q., Chen, Y., Li, C., & Shi, X. (2024). Carbon emission scenario prediction for highway construction projects. *Frontiers in Environmental Science, 11,* 1302220.

Zhang, Q., Li, X., Yu, L., Wang, L., Wen, Z., Su, P., … Wang, S. (2025). Machine learning-assisted fluorescence visualization for sequential quantitative detection of aluminum and fluoride ions. *Journal of Environmental Sciences, 149,* 68–78. https://doi.org/10.1016/j.jes.2024.01.023

Zhao, E., Wu, J., Wang, S., Sun, S., & Wang, S. (2024). Factors influencing energy consumption from China's tourist attractions: A structural decomposition analysis with LMDI and K-means clustering. *Environmental Modeling & Assessment, 29,* 569–587. https://doi.org/10.1007/s10666-023-09898-x

6

Future Directions and Innovation on Emerging Machine Learning Technologies in Environmental Science

Abstract

The integration of environmental sciences with cutting-edge approaches to data analysis like machine learning (ML) and artificial intelligence (AI) has led to a considerable evolution in monitoring and management of the environment (MME) as well as data analysis in the past few years. Improvements in data analytics are necessary to keep up with the daily surge in the amount and complexity of data collected in the environmental science domain. ML and other advanced data analysis techniques have become essential tools for uncovering hidden patterns or determining correlations that traditional analytical methods are unable to detect. Hence, via the quantitative analysis of relevant literature, this concluding chapter of this book will attempt to look at the future directions and innovation of emerging ML as well as AI-based technologies in environmental science. Enhancing data accessibility and quality, fostering cross-disciplinary collaboration between computer scientists and environmental scientists, and addressing some critical issues in emerging ML and AI-driven technologies in MME are the main focuses of future research. Consequently, highlighting the revolutionary potential of ML- and AI-based technologies for sustainable MME, providing insightful information that may assist researchers and policymakers in addressing the incessant environmental challenges facing the globe.

6.1 Introduction

Monitoring and management of the environment (MME) as well as data analysis have evolved significantly in recent years as a result of the integration of environmental sciences with advanced data analysis techniques (Hussain et al., 2024; Onyancha et al., 2021; Ukhurebor et al., 2021a, 2021b, 2022a, 2022b, 2024; Ukhurebor, Singh, Nayak, & UK-Eghonghon, 2021c) such

DOI: 10.1201/9781003618584-6

as artificial intelligence (AI) and machine learning (ML) (Alotaibi & Nassif, 2024; Olarte et al., 2025; Wang & Wu, 2024). By facilitating more precise predictions, real-time (RT) monitoring, and the analysis of enormous datasets that conventional techniques are unable to effectively handle, these technologies provide strong instruments to tackle difficult environmental issues (Alotaibi & Nassif, 2024; Olarte et al., 2025; Wang & Wu, 2024).

The global ecosystems and human health are seriously threatened by environmental issues like climate (CM) change, deforestation, pollution/contamination of the oceans, and biodiversity loss (Alotaibi & Nassif, 2024; Kerry et al., 2022; Olarte et al., 2025; Ukhurebor & Aidonojie, 2021; Wang & Wu, 2024). The implications of CM change, such as rising global temperatures, more frequent extreme weather events, and sea level rise, which endanger coastal ecosystems and humans (Ukhurebor, Azi, Aigbe, Onyancha, & Emegha, 2020) have been modelled using AI and ML, among other things (Alotaibi & Nassif, 2024; Olarte et al., 2025; Wang & Wu, 2024; Zhong et al., 2021).

AI-based models that evaluate images from satellites and identify illicit logging operations in RT have also been used widely to monitor deforestation, which is a key contributor to biodiversity loss and carbon emissions (Caesary, Kim, & Nam, 2025). AI-based tools have been utilized for detecting and tracking pollution/contamination in coastal waterways as well as the open sea, more efficiently discovering trends and sources of contamination. Ocean pollution/contamination, especially from plastic trash, poses serious threats to aquatic environments (Rana et al., 2023). The pressing need for creative solutions is highlighted by these environmental issues, and ML or AI approaches offer automated or computerized, effective, and scalable answers. AI models, for instance, are able to process vast amounts of data from sources like sensor (SS) networks, satellite imaging, and historical datasets, providing insights that had been previously impractical to obtain. AI-based applications in automated or computerized identification of species as well as MME are also addressing biodiversity loss by distributing vital data for conservation initiatives (Alotaibi & Nassif, 2024; Norouzzadeh et al., 2018; Villa et al., 2014).

The expanding amount of research showing the revolutionary potential of ML and AI in tackling these intricate environmental issues serves as the justification for this investigation. For example, ML-based algorithms have been used to accurately anticipate the effects of CM change, detect modifications to land use, and predict pollutant levels in the air. Similar to this, by offering accurate and useful information, AI-driven systems have improved the identification and control of environmental dangers, including spills of petroleum and burning forests (Cao, Han, Liu, & Li, 2025; Linardos, Drakaki, Tzionas, & Karnavas, 2022).

As a result of the swift progress and rising amount of research in this field, it is essential to conduct a comprehensive review of the current literature in order to pinpoint patterns, gaps, as well as potential avenues for further exploration. Hence, the last chapter of this book will attempt to look at the future directions and innovation in emerging ML as well as AI-based technologies in environmental science via the quantitative evaluation of scholarly literature. Awareness of the research landscape as well as the influences and contributions of various scholars, institutions, and nations can be expanded by looking at publishing outlines, citation networks, and trend in keywords. Review of previous studies/research on ML- and AI-based algorithms in MME and data analysis will be the main goal of this chapter.

6.2 A Brief Outline of Emerging ML- and AI-Based Technologies in MME

MME as well as data analysis are the two foremost domains that have been revolutionized by the currently developing fields of ML as well as AI. The development of systems that can carry out operations that normally demand human intelligence, like recognition of speech, perception of images, decision-making, and translation of languages, is included in the vast field of AI (Alotaibi & Nassif, 2024; Olarte et al., 2025; Wang & Wu, 2024). Developing algorithms that let computers learn from and make predictions or recommendations based on data is the main goal of ML, a branch of AI (Goodfellow, Bengio, & Courville, 2016; Nassif, Junaid, Altoubat, Maalej, & Barakat, 2024a; Nassif, Junaid, Hamad, Al-Sadoon, Altoubat, & Maale, 2024b).

The three main categories of ML algorithms used in MME are: "supervised learning (SL), unsupervised learning (UL), and reinforcement learning (RL)" (Alotaibi & Nassif, 2024; Olarte et al., 2025; Wang & Wu, 2024). Training a model on a labelled dataset – one in which every training example has an output label – is known as SL. This method works especially well for tasks like identifying different kinds of vegetation or plants in satellite photos or the prediction of the levels of air quality (AQ). Neural networks (NNs), support vector machines (SVM), and decision trees are examples of common techniques in SL (Omar et al., 2023, 2024; Russell & Norvig, 2021). On the other hand, UL works with unlabelled data. Determining the inherent structure of a collection of data points is the aim. This might be helpful for identifying abnormalities in data regarding the environment or grouping related sources of pollution/contamination. UL methods typically include algorithms like principal component analysis (PCA) and k-means clustering (Hastie, Tibshirani, & Friedman, 2009). In RL, an agent learns to make or carries out decisions by under taking certain tasks and getting rewarded or penalized. This method could be used to enhance MME plans as well as environmental sustainability, such as developing regulations to cut emissions or regulating natural resources responsibly (Sutton & Barto, 2018). Deep learning (DL), a branch of ML distinguished by multi-layered NNs (deep NNs), is another AI approach. These methods are especially effective at managing big datasets and intricate patterns, which makes them appropriate for applications like environmental remote sensing (RS) (Yuan et al., 2020) time-series prediction in CM data (Lecun, Bengio, & Hinton, 2015), as well as image identification in satellite imagery (Alotaibi & Nassif, 2024).

6.3 Applications of Emerging ML- and AI-Based Technologies in MME

The application and utilization of emerging ML- and AI-based technologies in MME has expanded and grown significantly (Alotaibi & Nassif, 2024; Olarte et al., 2025; Wang & Wu, 2024). These technologies have proven their adaptability and efficacy by being used in a variety of fields to address critical environmental challenges (Alotaibi & Nassif, 2024; Olarte et al., 2025; Wang & Wu, 2024). However, only a few reported studies have explicitly explored the application of emerging ML as well as AI-based technologies in MME, despite the fact that several literature reviews have been carried out to investigate the current state of these fields' research. The accelerating increase in reported publications and the expanding variety of application domains were highlighted in one noteworthy study that examined globally occurring developments in AI-based research (Bracarense, Bawack, Wamba, & Carillo, 2022). In order to identify important themes and significant research collaborations, a further investigation concentrated on the literature reviews of current CM change studies was conducted by Haunschild, Bornmann, and Marx (2016). These studies demonstrated the importance of analysis of literature in comprehending the changing dynamics of research and directing further studies.

Only a few of the literature reviews have examined particular subfields within the context of MME. For instance, the most influential nations, universities, and important research fields were emphasized in literature-based studies of applications for RS in MME (Wang et al., 2019; Zhuang, Liu, Nguyen, He, & Hong, 2013). Other studies identified research trends and future opportunities by examining the application of emerging ML as well as AI-based technologies in pollution/contamination of the environment (Liu, Lu, Zhang, Liu, & Jiang, 2022), water resource management (Kamyab et al., 2023), and identification of changes in RS (Shi, Zhang, Zhang, Chen, & Zhan, 2020). Still missing, though, is a thorough literature review that incorporates emerging ML- and AI-based technologies implementations across the wider range of MME. According to Alotaibi and Nassif (2024), this gap offers a chance to methodically evaluate the state of the field, spot new trends, and point out areas that require more research. The various applications of emerging ML- and AI-based technologies in MME as summarized from existing literature

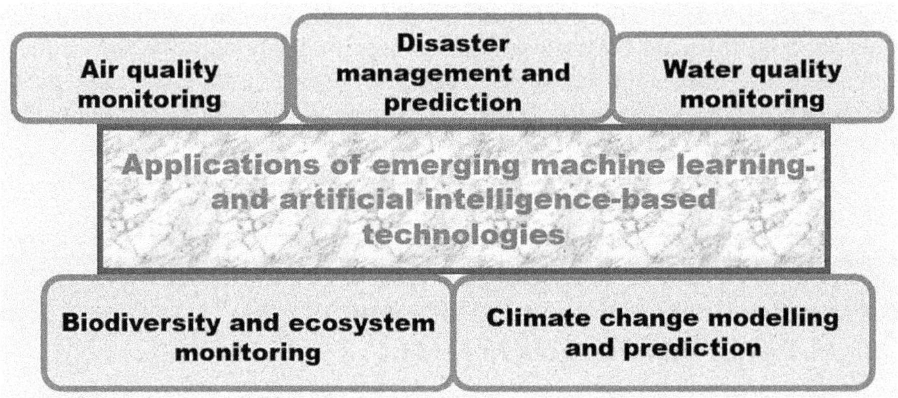

FIGURE 6.1
The various applications of emerging ML- and AI-based technologies in MME as summarized from existing literature.

(AQ monitoring, water quality (WQ) monitoring, CM change modelling and prediction, biodiversity and ecosystem monitoring, as well as disaster management and prediction (DMP)) are illustrated in Figure 6.1.

6.3.1 Applications of Emerging ML- and AI-Based Technologies in AQ Monitoring

AQ levels are predicted and tracked using emerging ML- and AI-based technologies. For example, emerging ML- and AI-based technologies can anticipate future levels of pollution/contamination by analysing meteorological variables along with previous air pollution/contamination data. Planning, management, and policy-making related to public health depend heavily on this data. Research has demonstrated that ensemble learning techniques and NNs can predict AQ with excellent accuracy (Grange, Lewis, & Carslaw, 2016; Vitolo, Scutari, Ghalaieny, Tucker, & Russell, 2018).

One crucial area where emerging ML- and AI-based technologies have shown tremendous potential is the monitoring of AQ. The geographical and temporal resolution required for thorough environmental assessments is frequently lacking in traditional AQ monitoring systems, which rely on permanent SSs that deliver data at specified locations (Scott, James, & Ali, 2006). By combining data from several sources, including satellite images, SS networks, and meteorological data, emerging ML as well as AI-based technologies algorithms have the potential to improve the monitoring of AQ by producing predictions that are more precise and timelier.

A Bayesian optimization approach was used by Cao et al. (2025) to forecast the levels of pollutants in metropolitan areas. Their research shows that ensemble models can increase the precision of quality of air predictions, especially in crowded urban locations, when used together with RT SS data. Model interpretability and prediction accuracy were enhanced by the fine-tuning of variables in the model made possible by the Bayesian optimization technique.

Utilizing random forest (RF) techniques, Chen et al. (2018) developed a model to estimate PM2.5 concentrations (CCNs) throughout China between 2005 and 2016. Their model demonstrated the potential of emerging ML- and AI-based technologies to reliably predict the quality of air over wide geographic areas by explaining 83.00% of the variability in PM2.5 CCNs.

In order to estimate PM2.5 CCNs in the US, Di et al. (2019) developed an ensemble model that used several emerging ML- and AI-based technologies. The model had a tenfold cross-validated R^2 between 0.86 and 0.89, indicating high accuracy. Their ensemble method shows how integrating several models can increase the accuracy as well as the generalizability of AQ predictions, especially in areas with different CMs.

In another recently conducted study on the global PM2.5 scale, Yu et al. (2023) used a deep ensemble ML (DEML) model for predicting daily PM2.5 CCNs globally between 2000 and 2019. This method achieved a high spatial resolution of 0.1° x 0.1° via the combination of chemical transport model outputs, meteorological data, as well as the ground-based measurements from 5,446 monitoring sites spread over 65 nations. With a "root mean square error (RMSE)" of 7.86 $\mu g/m^3$, the DEML model described 91.00% of the discovered variability in PM2.5 CCNs, offering comprehensive perceptions into patterns of the global exposure as well as the shifting spatiotemporal characteristics over a 20-year period. While population-weighted PM2.5 exposure decreased over time in geographic areas like Europe and North America, the study found notable regional differences, with increasingly elevated PM2.5 levels in South and East Asia, where over 90.00% of days in 2019 surpassed the daily PM2.5 limit of 15.00 $\mu g/m^3$ as recommended by the WHO. Because they provide scalable methods for AQ monitoring that can be used in a variety of geographical locations, these studies are especially pertinent to those involved in MME and policymakers.

This research indicates a number of difficulties even as it demonstrates the enormous potential of emerging ML- and AI-based technologies in AQ monitoring. For example, many models are still unable to account for the complexity of urban micro-CMs or predict devastating pollution/contamination events. Hence, as suggested by Alotaibi and Nassif (2024), future studies should focus on incorporating multi-scale sources of data, such as satellite data and ground-based SSs, in order to overcome these challenges and enhance the temporal and spatial resolution of quality of air projections. Furthermore, creating emerging ML- and AI-based models that are easier to understand may offer insightful information about the factors that contribute to air pollution/contamination, which would help urban policymakers as well as urban planners make better decisions. Researchers would be able to predict levels of pollution/contamination and comprehend the root causes with interpretable models, which is essential for creating more effective improvement in AQ measures.

6.3.2 Applications of Emerging ML- and AI-Based Technologies in WQ Monitoring

WQ indicators like pH, dissolved oxygen, and levels of contaminants have been evaluated and predicted using emerging ML- and AI-based technologies. In order to manage water resources and ensure usable, cleaner water, these models are able to handle data from SS networks and technologies for RS, offering accurate evaluations (Amani et al., 2020; Chen et al., 2020; Li et al., 2024; Maier et al., 2014; Rana et al., 2023).

Emerging ML- and AI-based technologies used in MME have shown great promise in WQ monitoring (Ndunagu, Ukhurebor, Akaaza, & Onyancha, 2022). Manual sampling and laboratory analysis are the mainstays of traditional WQ evaluation, which could be costly, time-consuming (slow), and logistically difficult, especially in remote (isolated) locations. By using data from SS networks and satellite imaging platforms, as well as historical datasets for predicting metrics of WQ in RT, emerging ML- and AI-based technologies have the ability to automate and improve these procedures.

Artificial neural networks (ANNs) were used by Palani, Liong, and Tkalich (2008) to predict the WQ of Singapore's coastal waterways. With "Nash–Sutcliffe coefficients" of efficiency between 0.80 and 0.90, the model proved good accuracy for prediction, indicating the efficacy of AI-based technologies in predicting important WQ metrics, including dissolved oxygen levels and fertilizer CCNs. Considering changes in WQ can have major ecological and economic effects, this study is especially pertinent to maintaining coastal habitats.

For the purpose of predicting the WQ of the Tualatin River, Lu and Ma (2020) presented a hybrid model that combines "extreme gradient boosting (XGBoost) and the Complete Ensemble Empirical Mode Decomposition with Adaptive Noise (CEEMDAN) approach". The potential benefits of mixing ML algorithms with signal processing techniques to increase the precision of environmental predictions were demonstrated by the hybrid model's superior performance over traditional models. Their methodological innovation – employing "empirical mode decomposition" to preprocess noisy WQ data before using ML algorithms – could be extended to other MME situations where datasets are noisy or inadequate.

For groundwater potential mapping in Iran, Naghibi, Pourghasemi, and Dixon (2016) used a variety of ML models, such as RF and "boosted regression trees (BRT)". According to their findings, the BRT model performed better than the other models in terms of accuracy in the predictions (predictive accuracy), indicating that ensemble learning approaches are a good fit for MME where integrating diverse information is necessary. For sustainable management of water resources, groundwater potential mapping is crucial, especially in arid and semi-arid areas where water is in short supply (Subbarayan, Thiyagarajan, Karuppannan, & Panneerselvam, 2024).

In a different study, Hill and Minsker (2010) used multilayer perceptron networks and autoregressive modelling to develop a RT anomaly detection algorithm for data related to the environment streams. Their approach demonstrated the potential of emerging ML- and AI-based technologies to improve the dependability of SS-based monitoring systems by detecting inaccurate data in the quality of water SSs and flagging anomalies in RT.

The research studies discussed here show how emerging ML- and AI-based technologies might enhance WQ monitoring, but they also point out a number of difficulties. For instance, a lot of models depend on RT, high-quality data, which can be difficult to access in areas with limited resources. Hence, Alotaibi and Nassif (2024) suggested that future studies should concentrate on creating reliable emerging ML- and AI-based technologies that can manage noisy or inadequate datasets and investigating how data fusion techniques may be used to combine data from many sources, including SS networks, satellite imaging, and historical datasets. Furthermore, more transparency and confidence in AI-based systems for the water management would be provided by the development of explainable emerging ML- and AI-based technologies, especially for regulation and policy-making circumstances.

6.3.3 Applications of Emerging ML- and AI-Based Technologies in CM Change Modelling and Prediction

In CM modelling, emerging ML- and AI-based technologies play a key role by simulating and forecasting climatic trends using vast amounts of data regarding the environment. Understanding the effects of CM change and designing mitigation and adaptation strategies are made easier with the use of these models (Hussain et al., 2024; Reichstein et al., 2019; Ukhurebor et al., 2024). Since traditional simulation models frequently have difficulty handling the complexity and volume associated with environmental data, emerging ML- and AI-based technologies have become more and more popular in the modelling and prediction of CM change. More precise projections of the effects of CM change and more informed choices about mitigation and adaptation measures are made possible by emerging ML- and AI-based technologies, which provides a potent tool for identifying trends and forecasting outcomes based on enormous volumes of historical CM (Alotaibi & Nassif, 2024; Olarte et al., 2025; Wang & Wu, 2024).

Reichstein et al. (2019) highlighted how DL methods can be used for the prediction of long-term modifications to the environment and model CM dynamics. Recurrent NNs and convolutional neural networks (CNNs) have the ability to model time series data and capture intricate spatiotemporal linkages in CM systems, as demonstrated by their study. This study provides a scalable method of CM modelling that might be used in many geographical locations and environmental circumstances by utilizing high-resolution satellite data and combining it with ground-based measurements.

Yu et al. (2023) used decision trees and NNs in developing a model for assessing the effects of CM change. In order to plan for adequate food supply in the face of shifting climatic trends, their model concentrated on predicting how CM change will affect yields from agriculture. The study demonstrated that emerging ML- and AI-based technologies could accurately forecast agricultural yields, providing agriculturalists and policymakers in CM change-vulnerable areas with a useful tool for decision-making.

Forzieri, Dakos, McDowell, Ramdane, and Cescatti (2022) made a significant addition to this field by combining RF models with satellite-based vegetation indicators to evaluate how resilient forests are to CM change. Their model had the capability to predict the long-term effects of several climatic scenarios on forest health and identify ecosystems that were at risk. Because it offers a scalable method of tracking the effects of CM change on ecosystems, this research is very pertinent to conservation initiatives and the management of biodiversity.

Modelling the effects of extreme weather occurrences, such as hurricanes, severe droughts, and flooding, is another application of emerging ML- and AI-based technologies. To illustrate the potential of these models for identifying vulnerable locations and assisting with mitigation procedures, Chapi et al. (2017) used ML algorithms to predict the vulnerability to flooding in Iran. Similarly, Gibb et al. (2019) employed AI-based technologies to evaluate satellite imagery and social media (SM) data in order to evaluate the immediate effects of hurricanes and assist disaster response agencies in making decisions.

There are still issues that need to be resolved even with the substantial advancements made in emerging ML- and AI-based technologies in CM modelling. The "black-box" nature of many ML models is one of the primary challenges, making it challenging to decipher the fundamental mechanisms guiding the predictions and interpreting the results that were obtained. Hence, Alotaibi and Nassif (2024) suggested that creating explainable ML- and AI-based technologies that shed light on the causes and effects of CM change should be the main goal of future research. To make sure that forecasts are based on accepted scientific theories and are more applicable to various locales and situations, further study is also required on the combination of emerging ML- and AI-based models with physical CM models.

6.3.4 Applications of Emerging ML- and AI-Based Technologies in Biodiversity and Ecosystem Monitoring

Emerging ML- and AI-based technologies are used for monitoring biodiversity and evaluating the condition of ecosystems, especially those that involve processing and recognizing images (Alotaibi & Nassif, 2024; Olarte et al., 2025; Wang & Wu, 2024). DL-based automated systems, for instance, can recognize and categorize species from camera trap photos, assisting in the long-term monitoring of biodiversity and wildlife populations (Norouzzadeh et al.

2018; Reichstein et al., 2019). Emerging ML- and AI-based technologies have been used with growing success in biodiversity monitoring images (Alotaibi & Nassif, 2024; Olarte et al., 2025; Wang & Wu, 2024). Monitoring biodiversity, evaluating the health of ecosystems, and tracking shifts in distributions of species and conditions of habitat are all being done with emerging ML- and AI-based technologies, especially those that involve picture recognition and data analysis. Compared to traditional monitoring approaches that frequently depend on human data gathering and have limited breadth and coverage, these methods provide scalable and effective alternative images (Alotaibi & Nassif, 2024; Olarte et al., 2025; Wang & Wu, 2024).

The Maxent algorithm, an ML method for species distribution modelling developed by Phillips, Aneja, Kang, and Arya (2006) has subsequently grown to be a popular instrument in biodiversity research. The study showed that when it comes to forecasting species ranges based on environmental characteristics, Maxent performs better than other algorithms, including the "Genetic Algorithm for Rule-set Production (GARP)". Because it enables scientists to forecast how distributions of species will alter in response to changing environmental modifications like loss of habitat and CM change, this research has important ramifications for planning for conservation and the management of biodiversity.

In order to monitor wildlife, Norouzzadeh et al. (2018) used DL algorithms to analyse camera trap photos. Their model greatly reduced the time and effort needed for the analysis of manual image by automatically identifying and classifying animal species with high accuracy. This strategy is especially pertinent for wildlife monitoring in isolated or difficult-to-reach locations where conventional techniques might not be feasible.

Similarly, Gonzalez et al. (2016) used AI-based technologies like object tracking and thermal imaging in combination with "unmanned aerial vehicles (UAVs)" to track populations of wildlife in forest ecosystems. Compared to conventional ground-based techniques, they were able to follow species in RT and detect changes in the population more accurately by combining AI-based technologies with UAVs. By offering RT data on the distribution of species and habitat settings, this multidisciplinary method shows how AI-based technologies can improve biodiversity monitoring.

Emerging ML- and AI-based technologies are being used for more than just tracking wildlife in biodiversity monitoring. The use of ML to improve fluorescence-based detection techniques for locating environmental pollutants that impact biodiversity, like aluminium and fluoride ions, was investigated by Zhang et al. (2025). Their model outperformed conventional approaches in terms of sensitivity and accuracy, demonstrating how AI-based technologies may enhance MME methods across a range of scenarios.

Even though this research demonstrates emerging ML- and AI-based technologies' important contributions to biodiversity monitoring, there are still some challenges. The requirement for sizeable, superior datasets to train ML models is one of the primary challenges. The absence of thorough biodiversity data in several locations, especially in the Global South, restricts the use of emerging ML- and AI-based technologies there. Hence, Alotaibi and Nassif (2024) suggested that future studies should concentrate on designing models that could function with unbalanced or limited datasets and investigating how data augmentation methods could enhance the performance of models in areas with little data.

6.3.5 Applications of Emerging ML- and AI-Based Technologies in DMP

In adverse event response and management, emerging ML- and AI-based technologies are essential. Natural disasters like hurricanes, flooding, and wildfires can be predicted by predictive models, allowing for allocation of resources and prompt responses. Emerging ML- and AI-based technologies can also help with SM data analysis to evaluate disaster impacts and plan response activities (Linardos et al., 2022). Emerging ML- and AI-based technologies have also been used in catastrophe prediction and management, where they provide notable advantages over conventional methods. Emerging ML- and AI-based models could make RT predictions of disasters that occur naturally such as hurricanes, flooding, and wildfires and assist disaster response agencies in making decisions by analysing vast volumes of data from several sources, including SS networks, SM, and satellite imagery (Alotaibi & Nassif, 2024).

The Bagging-LMT model was used by Chapi et al. (2017) for predicting Iran's vulnerability to flooding. Their approach was a useful tool for managing risks and DMP since it was more accurate than conventional techniques at identifying high-risk locations. The study shows how emerging ML- and AI-based technologies can be applied to improve DMP models' accuracy and give decision-makers useful information for allocating resources and making emergency plans.

In a different study, Linardos et al. (2022) designed a ML-based model which evaluates the effects of hurricanes in RT by combining SM data alongside satellite imagery. In order to determine the impacted locations and gauge the extent of the damage that occurred, their model was able to examine the geographic distribution of the SM posts. By offering RT, open-source information that could be utilized to guide emergency response plans, this method shows how emerging ML- and AI-based technologies may complement conventional DMP systems. Rapid and more precise evaluations of the effects of disasters are made possible by the combination of SM data alongside satellite imaging, which provides a more complete picture of the condition on the ground.

Gaussian Process Regression and Monte Carlo simulations were utilized by Uddin, Nash, Rahman, and Olbert (2023) to analyse uncertainty in WQ index (WQI) models during extreme events like flooding and tsunamis. Their model took into consideration the uncertainties present in data related to the environment, which is frequently noisy and lacking during disastrous situations, by combining probabilistic techniques with ML. When accuracy and time are critical in emergency situations, this method provides a strong framework for making well-informed decisions.

Another study conducted by Haridasan, Thomas, and Raj (2023) used principal component analysis (PCA) and CNNs to propose an automated approach for identifying and categorizing hazards caused by natural processes, such as earthquakes and landslides. High accuracy in prediction and RT processing proficiencies – both critical for disaster/catastrophe preparedness and response – were displayed by their system. Their algorithm was able to evaluate massive datasets in RT by utilizing AI-based technologies, giving responders to emergencies appropriate understanding and early warnings.

These studies demonstrate how emerging ML- and AI-based technologies have the potential to completely transform DMP by increasing prediction speed and accuracy and facilitating better emergency decision-making. But there are still a number of challenges. The scalability of emerging ML- and AI-based systems for DMP in many geographical locations is one of the primary obstacles. Since many models are trained using data specific to a given region, they could not generalize effectively to other places with differing socioeconomic and environmental circumstances. Hence, Alotaibi and Nassif (2024) suggest future studies should concentrate on developing more flexible models that may be used in a variety of geographical locations and crisis scenarios. Further investigation is also required on the ethical ramifications of applying emerging ML- and AI-based technologies to DMP, specifically with regard to concerns about data privacy as well as the possibility of bias in management as well as decision-making.

6.4 Methodological Advances in Emerging ML- and AI-Based Technologies for MME

There are several reported studies that have significantly advanced ML- and AI-based techniques designed for MME. These methodological developments include everything from the development of new algorithms to enhancing the scalability and interpretability of pre-existing models Alotaibi and Nassif (2024). The "Soil-Land Inference Model (SoLIM)", which integrates "geographic information systems (GIS)", expert knowledge, as well as fuzzy logic to enhance soil mapping capabilities, was first presented in a significant initial study by Zhu, Hudson, Burt, Lubich, and Simonson (2001). One example of how integrating AI with conventional environmental sciences might provide more precise and useful models is the merging of domain expertise with AI-based approaches. By increasing the resolution and accuracy of soil maps—that are essential for sustainable agriculture and land use planning—this study demonstrated how emerging AI-based technologies may improve soil and land management techniques (Hengl et al., 2017). A thorough meta-analysis of land-cover methods of classification was carried out by Khatami, Mountrakis, and Stehman (2016), with an emphasis on how adding texture data can increase accuracy in classifications. The study showed that when texture data is included, support vector machines perform better than other classification techniques. For RS applications, where land-cover classification is crucial for tracking modifications to the environment over time, this methodological advancement is especially pertinent.

The "Bagging-Logistic Model Tree (LMT) model" that integrates the "bagging ensemble technique and the LMT algorithm" for flood vulnerability mapping, was introduced in another important study by Chapi et al. (2017). Their findings demonstrated that by increasing prediction accuracy and lowering model bias, the hybrid model performed better than more conventional models like logistic regression and RF. In DMP, where precise and timely forecasts can aid in the allocation of resource as well as the mitigation of risk, this methodological advancement is essential.

A "dual-attention multiscale network (DAMFANet)" for detecting image changes from RS was proposed by Ren, Xia, Weng, Hu, and Lin (2024). The effectiveness of detection of changes algorithms is greatly enhanced by their model's inclusion of feature fusion and semantic information. This model provides a scalable and effective way to interpret RS images, addressing the prevalent problem of managing large-scale, heterogeneous data in MME. Prospects for AI-based applications in environmental research, especially in fields like land-use change detection and monitoring of deforestation, are made possible by the innovative technique of fusing attention machineries alongside multiscale feature learning.

When taken as a whole, these studies show important progress in emerging ML- and AI-based technologies for MME. These methodological advancements are assisting in bridging the gap between theoretical research and real-world applications by enhancing the models' accuracy and adaptability, as well as the ability for interpretation Alotaibi and Nassif (2024). Figure 6.2, as adapted from Alotaibi and Nassif (2024), summarizes the general publication patterns on the use of emerging ML- and AI-based technologies in MME from 1991 to 2024. A total of 4762 documents from 1580 sources were included in the analysis. 16,844 researchers published these articles, with an average of 5.08 co-authors per article. The fact that international co-authors appear in 30.24% of articles highlights this high degree of collaboration. According to their report, a total of 233,528 books were cited in these articles, demonstrating a thorough engagement with the literature as well as thorough research procedures. The influence of the study in this field was demonstrated by the average of 21.51 citations per document. The articles' 3.92-year average age indicates a recent and continuing emphasis on the use of ML- and AI-based technologies in MME.

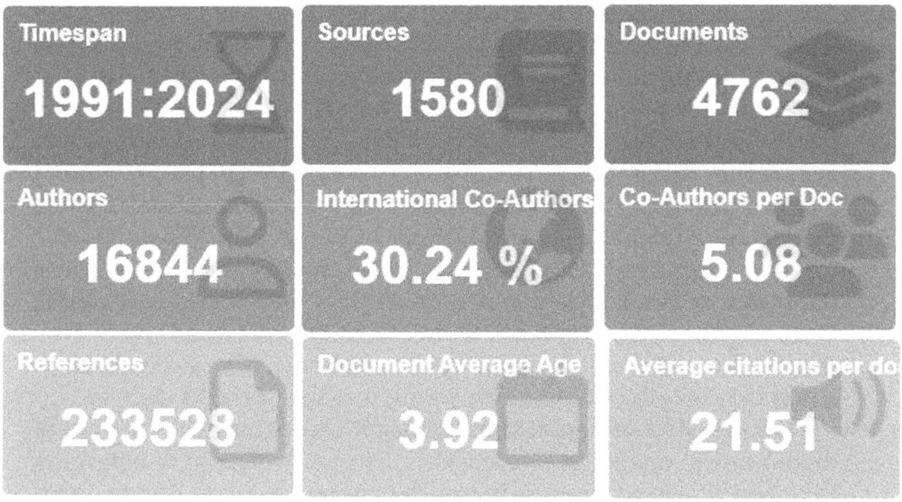

FIGURE 6.2
A summary of the general publication patterns on the use of ML- and AI-based technologies in MME from 1991 to 2024. (From Alotaibi and Nassif (2024), licensed under the CC BY 4.0 license.) (http://creativecommons.org/licenses/by/4.0/)

6.5 Future Directions on the Innovation of ML- and AI-based Applications for MME and Data Analysis

Recommendations for future directions of the innovation of ML as well as AI-based applications for MME and data analysis as adapted from the comprehensive review bibliometric analysis by Alotaibi and Nassif (2024) as well as other related studies are summarized as follows:

- Promoting multidisciplinary collaborations amongst academics from biomedical/health science, computer science, engineering/technology, physical sciences, and environmental science is essential to addressing the complicated issues of MME (Alotaibi & Nassif, 2024). These collaborations will result in more creative and comprehensive methods, guaranteeing that emerging ML- and AI-based applications have been tailored to address actual environmental issues from a variety of angles (Alotaibi & Nassif, 2024). For example, Asha et al. (2022) show how interdisciplinary/multidisciplinary efforts can produce RT monitoring solutions by successfully integrating IoT SSs with AI-based algorithms to monitor industrial air pollution/contamination. Similarly, Gonzalez et al. (2016) integrating AI-based wildlife monitoring devices with UAVs highlights the promise of interdisciplinary approaches in tackling intricate environmental problems like biodiversity loss.

- The availability and quality of data regarding the environment should be improved, especially in areas with limited resources. Several emerging ML- and AI-based models depend on vast amounts of high-quality data to work well, yet they may perform poorly in places with little access to data, such as rural or developing nations. The development of reliable ML- and AI-based technologies that can manage noisy, imperfect, or biased data should be the main goal of future research (Alotaibi & Nassif, 2024). These involve transfer learning strategies which could modify models for areas with poor or limited data and sophisticated data fusion algorithms that integrate data from many sources (Alotaibi & Nassif, 2024). This recommendation is supported by the study by Athanasoulias et al. (2024) that investigates the development of the "Plegma dataset" for improving environmental simulations. It shows how the creation of high-quality, open-access datasets can greatly enhance emerging ML- and AI-based monitoring of the environment in underserved areas. Additionally, Caesary et al. (2025) stress the need for enhancing the quality of data in economical ecological applications, offering a starting point for resolving data constraints in regions with limited resources.
- Despite having a strong predictive capacity, emerging ML- and AI-based models are frequently criticized for being "black-box" in nature. The confidence and uptake of AI-based technologies in MME, where choices could have major societal and ecological repercussions, may be restricted by this lack of transparency (Alotaibi & Nassif, 2024). To improve the transparency and interpretability of these models, more research on "explainable AI (XAI)" approaches is necessary. A wider implementation of these technologies in MME and decision-making will be made possible by improving stakeholders' trust in model processes for decision-making, which will benefit policymakers, academics, and the general public (Alotaibi & Nassif, 2024). The potential of XAI in MME and applications is demonstrated by studies like Lu and Ma (2020), which include explainable ML techniques in WQ prediction models, making the AI-based process for making decisions easier for end users to comprehend and act upon.
- Model accuracy and generalizability can be greatly increased by combining data-driven emerging ML- and AI-based technologies alongside domain-specific expertise, such as environmental guidelines in addition to physical models (Alotaibi & Nassif, 2024). Environmental simulations that are more thorough and comprehensible may be possible using hybrid models that include physics-based concepts in emerging ML- and AI-based systems. This integration will improve model robustness, especially for complicated environmental conditions like ecosystem dynamics and CM change. The initial study by

Zhu et al. (2001) that integrates fuzzy logic, expert knowledge, in addition to GIS in mapping of the soil, is an example of how hybrid models in environmental research can produce simulations that are more accurate and sensitive to context. In their use of hybrid AI models for flood prediction, Chapi et al. (2017) showed how integrating hydrological models and ML can enhance forecast accuracy and resilience in DMP.

- New capacities for monitoring of the environment are made possible by ongoing research into contemporary technologies, including advanced SSs, quantum computing, and innovative ML- and AI-based algorithms (Alotaibi & Nassif, 2024). These technologies can open up novel prospects for MME and prediction as well as RT, large-scale analysis of data. The fracking dynamics study by Anees et al. (2024), for instance, demonstrates the increasing demand for scalable AI-based models that could possibly process massive amounts of data in RT in order to efficiently control environmental concerns. In an earlier study, Asha et al. (2022) investigation of the integration of AI alongside the IoT shows how AI-based SS networks can provide scalable, RT MME technologies that could be used in a range of settings, from urban AQ monitoring to industrial pollution/contamination management.
- As emerging ML- and AI-based technologies become more and more integrated into MME, responsible emerging ML- and AI-based frameworks that put accountability, equity, and transparency first should be developed (Alotaibi & Nassif, 2024). Potential biases in emerging ML- and AI-based technologies should be addressed by researchers to make sure that these tools do not perpetuate current inequalities (Alotaibi & Nassif, 2024). Integrating ethical emerging ML- and AI-based technologies into MME is essential, especially for applications that impact ecosystems or communities that are at risk (Alotaibi & Nassif, 2024). Although extremely influential, Also, Phillips et al. (2006) in their study on the distribution models of species utilizing Maxent draws attention to the moral dilemmas associated with depending on opaque AI-based models, especially when conservation management and decision-making are involved. Future studies should make sure that AI-based models applied in these situations are not only precise but also ethical and accountable. Bias in AI-based systems should be avoided in areas with limited resources or availability of data since this could lead to unfair management of resource choices or distorted environmental predictions.
- The development of emerging ML- and AI-based technologies in the MME requires international cooperation and data exchange. Researchers can create models that are more broadly applicable and generalizable across many geographical locations and environmental

circumstances by facilitating access to environmental datasets and fostering international collaborations (Alotaibi & Nassif, 2024). The necessity for better data-sharing procedures is highlighted by the work by Cao et al. (2025), which tackles the worldwide scope of monitoring the AQ by means of cross-regional data integration. In a similar vein, Tamiminia et al. (2020) highlighted how international platforms such as "Google Earth Engine" can support the analysis of extensive environmental data, allowing for cross-national and multidisciplinary collaborations.

- CM change is making ecological catastrophes more frequent, which necessitates AI-based models that are both accurate and flexible enough to adjust to changing conditions in the environment (Alotaibi & Nassif, 2024). Developing emerging ML- and AI-based technologies that can instantly adapt to new data inputs in addition to the modifications in the environment should be the main goal of future research (Alotaibi & Nassif, 2024). The potential of these technologies to offer early warnings as well as lessen the effects of disasters/catastrophes that are occurring naturally is demonstrated by the use of emerging AI-based technologies in DMP, as demonstrated by Haridasan et al. (2023) for landslip detection as well as for the predictions of flooding as reported by Uddin, Nash, Rahman, and Olbert (2023). To ensure their continued applicability and efficacy, models should be able to adjust to novel disaster scenarios or unanticipated modifications to the environment.

6.6 Conclusion

This concluding chapter of this book has again emphasized the significant progress and transformative potential of ML as well as AI-based technologies in advancing MME in addition to analysis of data. The conclusions highlight the field's interdisciplinary/multidisciplinary nature and the global collaboration of researchers in tackling current environmental problems. In order to provide accurate and readily available data for decision-making, enable efficient mitigation techniques, and support sustainable MME practices, the integration of emerging ML- and AI-based technologies will be essential as the world faces urgent challenges like CM change, biodiversity loss, and depletion of resource. Despite notable progress, the use of emerging ML- and AI-based technologies in MME is still dynamic and continually developing. Harnessing the full potential of these innovations and helping to build a more ecologically resilient and sustainable future will require continuous research, innovation, and collaboration.

References

Alotaibi, E., & Nassif, N. (2024). Artificial intelligence in environmental monitoring: In-depth analysis. *Discover Artificial Intelligence, 4*(84). https://doi.org/10.1007/s44163-024-00198-1

Amani, M., Ghorbanian, A., Ahmadi, S. A., Kakooei, M., Moghimi, A., Mirmazloumi, S. M., ... Brisco, B. (2020). Google earth engine cloud computing platform for remote sensing big data applications: A comprehensive review. *The IEEE Journal of Selected Topics in Applied Earth Observations and Remote Sensing, 13,* 5326–5350. https://doi.org/10.1109/JSTARS.2020.3021052

Anees, A. A., Mehmood, K., Rehman, A., Rehman, N. U., Muhammad, S., Shahzad, F., ... Waseem Razzaq Khan, W. R. (2024). Unveiling fractional vegetation cover dynamics: A spatiotemporal analysis using MODIS NDVI and machine learning. *Environmental and Sustainability Indicators, 24,* 100485. https://doi.org/10.1016/j.indic.2024.100485

Asha, P., Natrayan, L., Geetha, B. T., Beulah, J. R., Sumathy, R., Varalakshmi, G., & Neelakandan, S. (2022). IoT enabled environmental toxicology for air pollution monitoring using AI techniques. *Environmental Research, 205,* 112574. https://doi.org/10.1016/j.envres.2021.112574

Athanasoulias, S., Guasselli, F., Doulamis, N., Doulamis, A., Ipiotis, N., Katsari, A., ... Stankovic, V. (2024). The Plegma dataset: Domestic appliance level and aggregate electricity demand with metadata from Greece. *Scientific Data*. https://doi.org/10.1038/s41597-024-03208-0

Bracarense, N., Bawack, R. E., Wamba, S. F., & Carillo, K. D. A. (2022). Artificial intelligence and sustainability: A bibliometric analysis and future research directions. *Pacific Asia Journal of the Association for Information Systems, 14*(2), 9. https://doi.org/10.17705/1pais.14209

Caesary, D., Kim, H., & Nam, M. J. (2025). Cost effectiveness of carbon capture and storage based on probability estimation of social cost of carbon. *Applied Energy, 377,* 124542. https://doi.org/10.1016/j.apenergy.2024.124542

Cao, H., Han, L., Liu, M., & Li, L. (2025). Spatial differentiation of carbon emissions from energy consumption based on machine learning algorithm: A case study during 2015–2020 in Shaanxi, China. *Journal of Environmental Sciences, 149,* 358–373. https://doi.org/10.1016/j.jes.2023.08.007

Chapi, K., Singh, V. P., Shirzadi, A., Shahabi, H., Bui, D. T., Pham, B. T., & Khosravi, K. (2017). A novel hybrid artificial intelligence approach for flood susceptibility assessment. *Environmental Modelling & Software, 95,* 229–245. https://doi.org/10.1016/j.envsoft.2017.06.012

Chen, G., Li, S., Knibbs, L. D., Hamm, N. A. S., Cao, W., Li, T., ... Guo, Y. (2018). A machine learning method to estimate PM2.5 concentrations across China with remote sensing, meteorological and land use information. *Science of the Total Environment, 636,* 52–60. https://doi.org/10.1016/j.scitotenv.2018.04.251

Chen, K., Chen, H., Zhou, C., Huang, Y., Qi, X., Shen, R., ... Ren, H. (2020). Comparative analysis of surface water quality prediction performance and identification of key water parameters using different machine learning models based on big data. *Water Research*. https://doi.org/10.1016/j.watres.2019.115454

Di, Q., Amini, H., Shi, L., Kloog, I., Silvern, R., Kelly, J., … Schwartz, J. (2019). An ensemble based model of PM2.5 concentration across the contiguous United States with high spatiotemporal resolution. *Environment International*. https://doi.org/10.1016/j.envint.2019.104909

Forzieri, G., Dakos, V., McDowell, N. G., Ramdane, A., & Cescatti, A. (2022). Emerging signals of declining forest resilience under climate change. *Nature, 608*(7923), 534–539. https://doi.org/10.1038/s41586-022-04959-9

Gibb, R., Browning, E., Glover-Kapfer, P., & Jones, K. E. (2019). Emerging opportunities and challenges for passive acoustics in ecological assessment and monitoring. *Methods in Ecology and Evolution, 10*(2), 169–185. https://doi.org/10.1111/2041-210X.13101

Gonzalez, L. F., Montes, G. A., Puig, E., Johnson, S., Mengersen, K., & Gaston, K. J. (2016). Unmanned aerial vehicles (UAVs) and artificial intelligence revolutionizing wildlife monitoring and conservation. *Sensors*. https://doi.org/10.3390/s16010097

Goodfellow, I., Bengio, Y., & Courville, A. (2016). *Deep learning*. Cambridge: MIT Press.

Grange, S. K., Lewis, A. C., & Carslaw, D. C. (2016). Source apportionment advances using polar plots of bivariate correlation and regression statistics. *Atmospheric Environment, 145*, 128–134. https://doi.org/10.1016/J.ATMOSENV.2016.09.016

Haridasan, A., Thomas, J., & Raj, E. D. (2023). Deep learning system for paddy plant disease detection and classification. *Environmental Monitoring and Assessment*. https://doi.org/10.1007/s10661-022-10656-x

Hastie, T., Tibshirani, R., & Friedman, J. (2009). The elements of statistical. Learning. https://doi.org/10.1007/978-0-387-84858-7

Haunschild, R., Bornmann, L., & Marx, W. (2016). Climate change research in view of bibliometrics. *PLoS One, 11*(7), e0160393. https://doi.org/10.1371/JOURNAL.PONE.0160393.

Hengl, T., De Jesus, J. M., Heuvelink, G. B. M., Gonzalez, M. R., Kilibarda, M., Blagotić, A., … Kempen, B. (2017). SoilGrids250m: Global gridded soil information based on machine learning. *PLoS One*. https://doi.org/10.1371/journal.pone.0169748

Hill, D. J., & Minsker, B. S. (2010). Anomaly detection in streaming environmental sensor data: A data-driven modeling approach. *Environmental Modelling & Software, 25*(9), 1014–1022. https://doi.org/10.1016/j.envsoft.2009.08.010

Hussain, A., Sipra, H. F. K., Waheed, A., & Ukhurebor, K. E. (2024). Exploring the academic perceptions of climate engineering in developing countries. *Atmósfera, 38*, 311–325.

Kamyab, H., Khademi, T., Chelliapan, S., SaberiKamarposhti, M., Rezania, S., Yusuf, M., … Ahn, Y. (2023). The latest innovative avenues for the utilization of artificial intelligence and big data analytics in water resource management. *Results in Engineering, 20*, 101566. https://doi.org/10.1016/J.RINENG.2023.101566

Kerry, R. G., Montalbo, F. J. P., Das, R., Patra, S., Mahapatra, G. P., Maurya, G. K., … Rou, J. R. (2022). An overview of remote monitoring methods in biodiversity conservation. *Environmental Science and Pollution Research, 2022*, 1–43.

Khatami, R., Mountrakis, G., & Stehman, S. V. (2016). A meta-analysis of remote sensing research on supervised pixel-based land-cover image classification processes: General guidelines for practitioners and future research. *Remote Sensing of Environment, 177*, 89–100. https://doi.org/10.1016/j.rse.2016.02.028

Lecun, Y., Bengio, Y., & Hinton, G. (2015). Deep learning. *Nature, 521*(7553), 436–444. https://doi.org/10.1038/nature14539

Li, X., Su, J., Wang, H., Boczkaj, G., Mahlknecht, J., Singh, S. V., & Wang, C. (2024). Bibliometric analysis of artificial intelligence in wastewater treatment: Current status, research progress, and future prospects. *Journal of Environmental Chemical Engineering, 12*(4), 113152. https://doi.org/10.1016/J.JECE.2024.113152

Linardos, V., Drakaki, M., Tzionas, P., & Karnavas, Y. L. (2022). Machine Learning in disaster management: Recent developments in methods and applications. *Machine Learning and Knowledge Extraction, 4*(2), 446–473. https://doi.org/10.3390/MAKE4020020

Liu, X., Lu, D., Zhang, A., Liu, Q., & Jiang, G. (2022). Data-driven machine learning in environmental pollution: Gains and problems. *Environmental Science & Technology, 56*(4), 2124–2133. https://doi.org/10.1021/acs.est.1c06157

Lu, H., & Ma, X. (2020). Hybrid decision tree-based machine learning models for short-term water quality prediction. *Chemosphere.* https://doi.org/10.1016/j.chemosphere.2020.126169

Maier, H. R., Kapelan, Z., Kasprzyk, J., Kollat, J., Matott, L. S., Cunha, M. C., … Reed, P. M. (2014). Evolutionary algorithms and other metaheuristics in water resources: Current status, research challenges and future directions. *Environmental Modelling & Software, 62*, 271–299. https://doi.org/10.1016/J.ENVSOFT.2014.09.013

Naghibi, S. A., Pourghasemi, H. R., & Dixon, B. (2016). GIS-based groundwater potential mapping using boosted regression tree, classification and regression tree, and random forest machine learning models in Iran. *Environmental Monitoring and Assessment, 188*(1), 1–27. https://doi.org/10.1007/s10661-015-5049-6

Nassif, N., Junaid, M. T., Altoubat, S., Maalej, M., & Barakat, S. (2024a). Data-driven prediction of the bond coefficient between fibre- reinforced polymer (FRP) bars and concrete. *Special Publication, 360*, 106–121.

Nassif, N., Junaid, M. T., Hamad, K., Al-Sadoon, Z., Altoubat, S., & Maalej, M. (2024b). Performance-based prediction of shear and flexural strengths in fiber-reinforced concrete beams via machine learning. *Structural Engineering International. 34*(6), 1–6.

Ndunagu, J. N., Ukhurebor, K. E., Akaaza, M. D., & Onyancha, R. B. (2022). Development of a wireless sensor network and IoT-based smart irrigation system. *Applied and Environmental Soil Science, 7678570*, 1–13.

Norouzzadeh, M. S., Nguyen, A., Kosmala, M., Swanson, A., Palmer, M. S., Packer, C., & Clune, J. (2018). Automatically identifying, counting, and describing wild animals in camera-trap images with deep learning. *Proceedings of the National Academy of Sciences of the United States of America, 115*(25), E5716–E5725. https://doi.org/10.1073/PNAS.1719367115

Olarte, E., Gutierrez, J., Roque, G., Soria, J. J., Fernandez, H., Carpio, J. E. P., & Poma, O. (2025). Predictive model with machine learning for environmental variables and PM2.5 in Huachac, Junín, Perú. *Atmosphere, 16*(3), 323. https://doi.org/10.3390/atmos16030323

Omar, M., Alotaibi, E., Arab, M. G., Shanableh, A., Malkawi, D. A. H., Elmehdi, H., & Tahmaz, A. (2023). Harnessing natureinspired soft computing for reinforced soil bearing capacity prediction: A neuro-nomograph approach for efficient design. *International Journal of Geosynthetics and Ground Engineering, 9*(4), 53.

Omar, M., Arab, M. G., Alotaibi, E., Alshibli, K. A., Shanableh, A., Elmehdi, H., … Tahmaz, A. (2024). Natural soils' shear strength prediction: A morphological data-centric approach. *Soils and Foundations, 64*(6), 101527. [CrossRef][10.1016/j.sandf.2024.101527]

Onyancha, R. B., Ukhurebor, K. E., Aigbe, U. O., Osibote, O. A., Kusuma, H. S., Darmokoesoemo, H., & Balogun, V. A. (2021). A systematic review on the detection and monitoring of toxic gases using carbon nanotube-based biosensors. *Sensing and Bio-Sensing Research, 34*, 100463.

Palani, S., Liong, S. Y., & Tkalich, P. (2008). An ANN application for water quality forecasting. *Marine Pollution Bulletin, 56*(9), 1586–1597. https://doi.org/10.1016/j.marpolbul.2008.05.021

Phillips, S. B., Aneja, V. P., Kang, D., & Arya, S. P. (2006). Modelling and analysis of the atmospheric nitrogen deposition in North Carolina. *International Journal of Global Environmental Issues, 6*(2–3), 231–252. https://doi.org/10.1016/j.ecolmodel.2005.03.026

Rana, R., Kalia, A., Boora, A., Alfaisal, F. M., Alharbi, R. S., Berwal, P., … Qamar, O. (2023). Artificial intelligence for surface water quality evaluation, monitoring and assessment. *Water, 15*(22), 3919. https://doi.org/10.3390/W15223919

Reichstein, M., Camps-Valls, G., Stevens, B., Jung, M., Denzler, J., Carvalhais, N., & Prabhat, N. (2019). Deep learning and process understanding for data driven earth system science. *Nature, 566*(7743), 195–204. https://doi.org/10.1038/s41586-019-0912-1

Ren, H., Xia, M., Weng, L., Hu, K., & Lin, H. (2024). Dual-attention-guided multiscale feature aggregation network for remote sensing image change detection. *The IEEE Journal of Selected Topics in Applied Earth Observations and Remote Sensing, 17*, 4899–4916. https://doi.org/10.1109/JSTARS.2024.3362370

Russell, S., & Norvig, P. (2021). *Artificial intelligence: A modern approach*. 4th ed. Hoboken: Pearson.

Scott, S. M., James, D., & Ali, Z. (2006). Data analysis for electronic nose systems. *Microchimica Acta, 156*(3–4), 183–207. https://doi.org/10.1007/s00604-006-0623-9

Shi, W., Zhang, M., Zhang, R., Chen, S., & Zhan, Z. (2020). Change detection based on artificial intelligence: State-of-the-art and challenges. *Remote Sensing, 12*(10), 1688. https://doi.org/10.3390/rs12101688

Subbarayan, S., Thiyagarajan, S., Karuppannan, S., & Panneerselvam, B. (2024). Enhancing groundwater vulnerability assessment: Comparative study of three machine learning models and five classification schemes for Cuddalore district. *Environmental Research*. https://doi.org/10.1016/j.envres.2023.117769

Sutton, R. S., & Barto, A. G. (2018). *Reinforcement learning: An introduction*. 2nd ed. Cambridge: MIT Press.

Tamiminia, H., Salehi, B., Mahdianpari, M., Quackenbush, L., Adeli, S., & Brisco, B. (2020). Google earth engine for geo-big data applications: A meta-analysis and systematic review. *The ISPRS Journal of Photogrammetry and Remote Sensing, 164*, 152–170. https://doi.org/10.1016/j.isprsjprs.2020.04.001

Uddin, M. G., Nash, S., Rahman, A., & Olbert, A. I. (2023). A novel approach for estimating and predicting uncertainty in water quality index model using machine learning approaches. *Water Research*. https://doi.org/10.1016/j.watres.2022.119422

Ukhurebor, K. E., & Aidonojie, P. A. (2021). The influence of climate change on food innovation technology: Review on topical developments and legal framework. *Agriculture & Food Security, 10*(50), 1–14.

Ukhurebor, K. E., Aigbe, U. O., Onyancha, R. B., Nwankwo, W., Osibote, O. A., Paumo, H. K., … Siloko, I. U. (2021a). Effect of hexavalent chromium on the environment and removal techniques: A review. *Journal of Environmental Management, 280,* 111809.

Ukhurebor, K. E., Aigbe, U. O., Onyancha, R. B., UK-Eghonghon, G., Balogun, V. A., Egielewa, P. E., ... Darmokoesoemo, H. (2022a). Greenhouse gases emission: Perception during the COVID-19 pandemic. *BioMed Research International, 6166276,* 1–12.

Ukhurebor, K. E., Aigbe, U. O., Onyancha, R. B., Athar, H., Okundaye, B., Aidonojie, P. A., ... Darmokoesoemo, H. (2024). Environmental influence of gas flaring: Perspective from the Niger Delta Region of Nigeria. *Geofluids, 1321022,* 1–17.

Ukhurebor, K. E., Azi, S. O., Aigbe, U. O., Onyancha, R. B., & Emegha, J. O. (2020). Analysing the uncertainties between reanalysis meteorological data and ground measured meteorological data. *Measurement, 165,* 108110.

Ukhurebor, K. E., Hussain, A., Adetunji, C. O., Aigbe, U. O., Onyancha, R. B., & Abifarin, O. (2021b). Environmental implications of petroleum spillages in the Niger delta region of Nigeria: A review. *Journal of Environmental Management, 293,* 112872.

Ukhurebor, K. E., Onyancha, R. B., Aigbe, U. O., UK-Eghonghon, G., Kerry, R. G., Kusuma, H. S., ... Balogun, V. A. (2022b). A methodical review on the applications and potentialities of using nanobiosensors for diseases diagnosis. *BioMed Research International, 1682502,* 1–20.

Ukhurebor, K. E., Singh, K. R. B., Nayak, V., & UK-Eghonghon, G. (2021c). Influence of SARS-CoV-2 pandemic: A review from the climate change perspective. *Environmental Science: Processes & Impacts, 23,* 1060–1078.

Villa, F., Bagstad, K. J., Voigt, B., Johnson, G. W., Portela, R., Honzak, M., & Batker, D. (2014). A methodology for adaptable and robust ecosystem services assessment. *PLoS One.* https://doi.org/10.1371/journal.pone.0091001

Vitolo, C., Scutari, M., Ghalaieny, M., Tucker, A., & Russell, A. (2018). Modeling air pollution, climate, and health data using bayesian networks: A case study of the English regions. *Earth and Space Science, 5*(4), 76–88. https://doi.org/10.1002/2017EA000326

Wang, L., Zhang, G., Wang, Z., Liu, J., Shang, J., & Liang, L. (2019). Bibliometric analysis of remote sensing research trend in crop growth monitoring: A case study in China. *Remote Sensing, 11*(7), 809. https://doi.org/10.3390/RS11070809

Wang, Y.-G., & Wu, J. (2024). Foreword: Machine Learning in environmental modelling. *Environmental Modeling & Assessment, 29,* 425–426. https://doi.org/10.1007/s10666-024-09981-x

Yu, W., Ye, T., Zhang, Y., Xu, R., Lei, Y., Chen, Z., ... Li, S. (2023). Global estimates of daily ambient fine particulate matter concentrations and unequal spatiotemporal distribution of population exposure: A machine learning modelling study. *Lancet Planet Health, 7,* e209.

Yuan, Q., Shen, H., Li, T., Li, Z., Li, S., Jiang, Y., ... Zhang, L. (2020). Deep learning in environmental remote sensing: Achievements and challenges. *Remote Sensing of Environment.* https://doi.org/10.1016/j.rse.2020.111716

Zhang, Q., Li, X., Yu, L., Wang, L., Wen, Z., Su, P., ... Wang, S. (2025). Machine learning-assisted fluorescence visualization for sequential quantitative detection of aluminum and fluoride ions. *Journal of Environmental Sciences, 149,* 68–78. https://doi.org/10.1016/j.jes.2024.01.023.

Zhong, S., Zhang, K., Bagheri, M., Burken, J. G., Gu, A., Li, B., … Zhang, H. (2021). Machine learning: New ideas and tools in environmental science and engineering. *Environmental Science & Technology, 55*(19), 12741–12754. https://pubs.acs.org/doi/10.1021/acs.est.1c01339

Zhu, A. X., Hudson, B., Burt, J., Lubich, K., & Simonson, D. (2001). Soil mapping using GIS, expert knowledge, and fuzzy logic. *Soil Science Society of America Journal.* https://doi.org/10.2136/sssaj2001.6551463x

Zhuang, Y., Liu, X., Nguyen, T., He, Q., & Hong, S. (2013). Global remote sensing research trends during 1991–2010: A bibliometric analysis. *Scientometrics, 96*(1), 203–219. DOI: 10.1007/s11192-012-0918-z

Index

Note: **Bold** and *italic* page numbers refer to **tables** and figures, respectively.

For Product Safety Concerns and Information please contact our EU
representative GPSR@taylorandfrancis.com
Taylor & Francis Verlag GmbH, Kaufingerstraße 24, 80331 München, Germany

www.ingramcontent.com/pod-product-compliance
Ingram Content Group UK Ltd.
Pitfield, Milton Keynes, MK11 3LW, UK
UKHW021507240926
475702UK00035B/652

* 9 7 8 1 0 4 1 0 2 1 9 7 1 *